Your Wedding FILE
TODAY

WENDY HOBSON

foulsham
LONDON • NEW YORK • TORONTO • SYDNEY

foulsham

The Publishing House
Bennetts Close, Cippenham,
Berkshire, SL1 5AP, England

ISBN 0-572-02427-4

Copyright © 1999 W. Foulsham & Co. Ltd

Research information provided by
Linda Tsiricos and Carole Chapman

The vast majority of companies with whom you
are likely to deal when organising your wedding
are reputable and professional. However, you
should always take steps to ensure that this is
the case.

Printed in Great Britain by St Edmundsbury Press, Bury St Edmunds, Suffolk

CONTENTS

Photograph Acknowledgements

With thanks to the following companies for allowing us to use their photographs in the book.

Adrienne Kerr Designs, Thai House, 5 Ravelston Terrace, Edinburgh, EH4 3EF (0131 332 5393)

Affectionately Yours Ltd, Chapel Hall, Downs Row, Rotherham, South Yorkshire, S60 2HD (01709 513551)

Ages Past, Warbrook Lane, Eversley, Hampshire, RG27 0PJ (0118 973 2630)

Bride Print, Unit 1, Gateside Industrial Estate, Lesmahagow, Lanarkshire, ML11 0JR (01555 895559)

Buttercup Couture, The Wedding Gallery, 17a Angel Road, Norwich, NR3 3HL (01603 612993)

Cambridge Omnibus and Carriage Hire, 28 St Audreys Close, Histon, Cambridge, CB4 4JX (01233 137395)

Danceland Shoe Company, 4 The Midway, Newcastle, Staffordshire, ST5 1QG (01782 635515)

Dunn's, 6 The Broadway, Crouch End, London, N8 9SN

Ellis Bridals, 1 Guillemot Place, Clarendon Road, London, N22 4QX. Gowns are from current ranges and are subject to availability. Telephone 0181 888 8833 for stockists.

Eternally Fresh, 2 The Royal Seafront, Hayling Island, Hampshire, PO11 0AD (01705 460236)

Hatstop, The Gallery, Pennybank Chambers, 33–5 St John's Square, London EC1M 4DS (0171 251 8490)

Haydn Webb Carriages, Lambs Farm Stables, Spencers Wood, Reading, Berkshire, RG7 1PH (0118 988 3334)

Lavender Green, 16 Park Street, Windsor, Berkshire (01753 831112)

Moss Bros Group plc, 8 St John's Hill, London, SW11 1SA (0171 447 7200)

Oakdene Stationery, 55 Gatehill Gardens, Luton, Bedfordshire, LU3 4EZ (01582) 585014)

Yellow Door Studio, 19 Upper Market Street, Hove, Sussex, BN3 1AS (01273 720660)

INTRODUCTION

Planning a wedding is a time-consuming and complicated process. You and your back-up team have a whole host of jobs to do, problems to solve and decisions to make – and that can be more than a little daunting as you start out on your route to the big day. At the moment you'll have more questions than answers. What are the first questions to resolve? How can I be sure I won't forget anything? Where do I find the best photographers? How much time will it all take? *Who is going to help me with all this?!*

The crucial thing to remember is that this is your day. There are plenty of etiquette guidelines, you know how your friends have planned their big days, you probably know roughly what is expected. But all that is only of any consequence if it matters to *you*. You are planning a celebration to mark a wonderful day which you and your partner will remember for the rest of your lives. You want it to be special – and you want it to be unique. The way to achieve that is to follow an organised and structured path towards your goal, making decisions as you proceed, discarding information that you do not need, weighing up the various options and deciding what you want – and wasting as little time and effort in the process as possible.

So how will a wedding file help me to organise my wedding?

Quite simply, it provides you with a blueprint for your wedding organisation. No two weddings are ever the same – and you certainly don't want yours to be the same as anyone else's – so we have laid down the groundwork, asked the right questions, pointed you in the direction of finding the perfect answers for you, so that you move logically through your planning to a successful conclusion. It will help you to make the best possible use of your time and the resources available and get the best possible results.

Who is this wedding file designed for?

It is perfect for the bride, the bride's mother, the groom –
for anyone who is involved in organising a wedding. It can
be a small and personal ceremony in a register office or a
grand event in a cathedral; a quiet drink with a few close
friends or a reception for a hundred guests in the grounds
of a stately home. Whoever you are and whatever you are
planning, this book will help you.

How is this planner unique?

In every wedding organiser, there is an element of overlap
between the various topics you have to consider. For
example, you need to think about the flowers when you are
making the plans for the church, the bridesmaids and the
reception. The essential point is that nothing is missed –
otherwise you'll have to go back over the same ground –
and the key to keeping everything in order is to design
your checklists around the *people* who matter. What do you
need to ask the vicar or registrar? Have you remembered
everything you want the florist to supply?

Your *Wedding File* is a people-based book – because it is
the people who get things done. Each section gives the
essential planning information you need in note form so
that it is accurate, straightforward and to the point. In this
way, you have a checklist of things to do or questions to
ask, depending on what is appropriate to that area of
planning.

When do I start?

Asking 'How long do different people take to plan their
wedding?' is a bit like asking 'How long is a piece of
string?' And the answer matters even less. The important
questions are 'When do we want to get married?' and
'How much time do we have to make the arrangements?'
Once those questions are settled, you can work on the
organisation for the event as quickly or at as leisurely a
pace as suits you. If you are reading this, you will already
know that starting early can have its advantages: you can
be sure of being able to book your first choice of suppliers
and dates, for example. But not everyone is able, or wants,
to plan too far ahead. As long as the sequence is logical, the
speed is up to you.

How do I use my wedding file?

The first few sections give you a general outline of what needs to be done and who, traditionally, is responsible for doing it. Each chapter in the book is then devoted to one of the key players in your wedding plans. The short introduction will give you an outline of the coverage of the chapter, then you have a series of sequential checklists to guide you through the essential elements of the planning of that particular aspect of the wedding. At the end of the chapter, there are more checklists so that you can fill in all the information you have accumulated: addresses of suppliers, reminder dates when you have to contact them again, guest lists and so on. Everything will then be safely stored in your own wedding file, ready and waiting for when you need it.

Will I have a perfect wedding?

With the help of *Your Wedding File*, you will be able to enjoy your wedding preparations because you will feel in control. However long you have to make your plans, you'll have a clear view of that perfect day in your sights and be able to head straight for it, confident that you will make it a day to remember.

introduction

Congratulations – you are engaged to be married. You have recovered from the engagement party and sent the announcement to the newspaper. Now you have to begin to plan the wedding day.

The first question most people ask when they start to plan a wedding is: 'Where do I start?' and the temptation is to answer: 'At the top and work downwards'! There is a lot to do when organising a wedding which you obviously want to be a very special day. As with anything involving multi-layered organisation, the key is in having a well-defined objective and a structured plan to get you there.

The Objective

So what is your objective? Although the details will vary with every wedding, everyone reading this book has the same basic objective. They have decided to get married, to commit themselves to the person they love, and they want to celebrate that event in the most wonderful and memorable way. Hang on to that thought throughout the next few months of planning, budgeting, choosing – and inevitable stresses and arguments.

You and your partner and the sort of celebration you want are what really matters. Of course you have to consider your family and friends and there will be compromises to be made to keep other people happy. Of course you have to think about your budget and you'll perhaps have to leave out some of the elements you would ideally have liked to include. But don't be fooled by the advertisers into thinking that the more you spend, the better the day will be. The day can be wonderful whatever you are able to spend – and you can make it so.

Take a blank sheet of paper and write 'My Wedding' at the top. Don't worry about details – three bridesmaids or two doesn't matter at the moment – but write down the things that are absolutely essential to making your day special. Take your time; think about it over a couple of days; talk about it with your partner or your mum; muse on it in the bath; keep going back to it until you are satisfied with what you have written. It may only be a few

the planning

sentences; it may be a fairly long list – either way, it should only include what is fundamental to you.

What you have written down is your blueprint for the day and should guide you in your decisions. Keep referring back to it – especially when things are not going to plan. One couple may decide they want to drink vintage champagne from cut-glass flutes all afternoon – so perhaps the bride will make her own dress, they'll borrow a friend's car to drive to the reception and invite just their closest family and friends to the reception. Another couple may have put 'brilliant sunshine' at the top of the list. Well, if you are British, that has to mean a wedding-package holiday and you may have to compromise on who will be able to attend. Perhaps you wrote, 'I want my sister to be able to come to the wedding' and that means a ticket from Australia. Change anything else, make savings anywhere else, but stick to what you really want.

The Structured Plan

So what about the plan? You are holding it in your hands! *Your Wedding File* cannot, of course, do everything for you because your wedding is going to be totally unique to you and you will be making all the crucial decisions, but it can show you which decisions need to be made at which stage, who can help you make them, and guide you into making the choices that are right for you.

Because there is always an overlap between different elements of the planning – you need to talk to the vicar and the florist about the church flowers, for example – it is a good idea to read through this book first to give you an idea of everything that is likely to be involved before you start working through in a logical way. Use *Your Wedding File* as a workbook, writing in personal information, crossing out sections that don't apply, personalising lists and really making it *Your Wedding File*. Then decide on a safe place to keep it! Buy yourself a concertina file or ring binder and alphabetical file dividers as well to keep all your booking letters and information tidy and easily accessible. Put your 'My Wedding' sheet at the front and look at it every time you open the file to make sure you are on track. Just establishing those simple organisational rules will take away a lot of hassle and make life much easier over the next few months.

Your Wedding File includes all the various elements

involved in organising a wonderful wedding, from booking the ceremony venue to returning the hired suits. At each stage, there will be some aspects that apply to you and some that don't. You can personalise the planning notes as you go along. This book is organised around the important people involved in the planning: from the vicar or registrar to the photographer and dressmaker. In addition to this, there is information on the appropriate timing (see Chapter 3), so that you are forewarned to make sure, for example, that you book your reception venue in good time.

Making the Crucial Decisions

In any business or organisation, communication is vital, so it is a good idea to start as you mean to go on by involving important people in your wedding plans and getting their support and co-operation – and hopefully some hard work out of them as well.

You will probably already have talked with the groom about whether you want a quiet civil ceremony and an intimate dinner, or a huge church affair and a riotous party. If not, now is the time to do it! This is an occasion to cement your relationship and, as such, should be something which will please both of you and allow both of you to include those individual touches which will make the day unique. Talk about all the options: the venues, the size of the guest list, how much you are able to spend, the best man and bridesmaids, the clothes. If you have unusual ideas, air them now – even if you are not able to take them up, at least you'll never think, 'I wish I'd asked if he'd like to …'.

Especially if your parents have not met your partner's parents before, arrange a dinner or get-together in a relaxed atmosphere so that they have a chance to get to know each other a little better; it will make the whole thing more cordial from the word go. Use that evening to discuss the type of wedding you would like and make sure everyone is happy with the implications. Think about the timing, the place and the scale of the event. Consider whether a number of people would have to travel considerable distances. If there is likely to be a gap between the end of the reception and the beginning of an evening party, what are the guests going to do? Get a feel for the whole day.

This is also a good time to discuss the timing of the

wedding. Does it have to coincide with specific times you can take off work? Are you thinking of a summer or a winter wedding? If one set of parents goes away at specific times of the year, these need to be avoided, as do times when you or the groom have business trips. Or perhaps you have a business trip planned which you could extend in order to save money on your honeymoon expenses!

Think as well about local events. Is the date you have in mind the day of the local marathon or carnival procession?

If you are planning well in advance, you should not need back-up dates as you will have the best choice of venues and services. If you don't have as much planning time, you'll have to decide whether the date or the ceremony venue is the crucial factor and change one or other accordingly if there are any problems.

The Wedding Party

The most important people at your wedding will be those closest to you, both family and friends. The first choices you need to make are which of your friends or relatives you are going to ask to make up your wedding party. If you know there is anything controversial in your choices, discuss it and find a way to resolve it at this stage. If the groom is determined to have as his best man a friend his mother refuses to speak to, you still have time to mend fences rather than endure icy stares between them which will chill your wedding-day sunshine!

Keep a note of the names and addresses of the wedding party on the reference sheet at the end of this chapter so they are always ready to hand when you need them.

It is traditional for the bride and groom to give gifts to the best man, bridesmaids and other attendants to thank them for their support during the planning stages and on the day itself. Try to make your choices personal ones. I know one best man who was slightly disappointed to receive a gift of a tablecloth and matching napkins!

The Bride's and Groom's Parents

Both sets of parents are going to be vital in the planning and preparation and on the big day itself. Usually the bride's father escorts the bride to the church to 'give her away' to the groom. If your father is not able to do this, you would normally ask an uncle, elder brother or close friend of the family. A civil ceremony does not include a 'giver-away'. The bride's parents also generally act as host and hostess of the occasion, so if this is not appropriate to your circumstances, the wedding may either be hosted by someone else close to you, or by you and the groom yourselves.

If either set of parents is divorced, it is helpful if you are able to clarify how the costs and responsibilities will be shared.

The Best Man

The role of the best man is as the groom's right-hand man, so he is usually a brother or close friend of the groom. Make sure you ask the best man in good time and do be sure that he is happy to take on the duties. Most men will be flattered, if a little terrified – usually at the thought of making the speech. Chat through what you expect, reassure him that you know he'll do an excellent job even if he doubts it himself, and buy him a copy of *Mitch Murray's One-liners for Weddings* (W. Foulsham & Co. Ltd) to help him with his speech. The groom and the bride's father can take a look at it as well.

If there is more than one contender for the job, you will have to make a decision and stick with it. Speak with the other friend to make sure that he is not offended and perhaps find him another role for the wedding day if that is appropriate.

The Chief Bridesmaid

As the best man looks after the groom, so the chief bridesmaid looks after the bride and is usually a sister or close friend. If you have two sisters or special friends, there is no need to choose between them, just dispense with the 'chief'.

The Bridesmaids and Page Boys

One of the potential problems here is that once you have chosen one niece or nephew and the son or daughter of a close friend, do you then ask all the others with the same relationship and end up with more attendants than wedding guests? Be realistic. You can only do your best to keep the whole world happy.

You may also like to appoint a flower girl, a girl usually

the planning

under eight years old who spreads flowers before you as you walk down the aisle. A boy of a similar age sometimes acts as a ring-bearer, carrying the rings on an ornate cushion.

The Ushers

This is not an onerous job and brothers and male relations and friends are usually happy to help out as ushers as it is a compliment to their friendship with the groom. Three is plenty for an average-sized wedding, but be guided by common sense. The best man and the groom can appoint a chief usher to undertake any special duties or stand in for the best man, for example so that he can leave the church to join the receiving line at the reception but still be assured that none of the guests will be left behind.

Other Attendants

If either of you has a military or police background or is a member of a club or organisation, you might like to ask one of these organisations to form a guard of honour as you leave the ceremony.

Talking about Money

Many people – especially the British – are reluctant to talk about money in family circumstances, but weddings can be expensive occasions and there is no getting away from this fact. An 'average' wedding in the UK in the late 1990s costs £8,000. Frightened? You should be! Needless to say, it does not have to cost that much, but I quote the figure to emphasise how important it is that you get to grips with the budget before you start.

Grit your teeth, take a deep breath and raise the subject. Be positive by starting with how much you can contribute to the cost of the wedding. If you have already been talking about the kind of day you would like it to be, the other members of the family will instantly know what kind of shortfall there is. They will already have thought about how much they might be able to spend before they arrived at your dinner party, so you will have a good 'guesstimate' of whether the income matches the sort of outgoings you have in mind.

If they roughly match up, that's fine – you can go ahead with your planning. If it looks as though you have far more money than you need – be cautious! You may have underestimated the cost of suppliers and services. In any event, there's no point in spending money for the sake of it. Perhaps your generous parents might put some money towards the honeymoon, a washing machine or the deposit on your house or flat. If the bad news is that you know already you have to moderate your plans to fit a tighter budget than you had hoped, be realistic and go back to your priorities. Why did you want to spend that much in the first place? What is really important? Celebrating your love and your commitment is what it is all about, after all, not getting into debt and creating unnecessary stress. You will have an utterly wonderful day whatever you are able to spend – you can do it!

Window-shopping

Especially if you have never been involved in planning a wedding before – for a sister or friend, for example – you are likely to be out of touch with the range of services and supplies available or exactly how much they cost. Take a notebook and go window-shopping in wedding suppliers; buy a couple of wedding magazines and send off for some brochures that interest you; perhaps attend a wedding exhibition. You can request free information from National Wedding Information Services (see page 187) and there are more contact numbers on pages 185–8. Ask around for recommendations from friends or relatives.

Armed with all this information, you are in the perfect position to start working out your actual plans and finalising the budget breakdown.

Insurance

Sometimes things do go wrong, and it is worth considering taking out wedding insurance. A broker will give you full information, or you can ask the National Wedding Information Services (see page 187). You can include cancellation of the ceremony or reception venue, loss or damage to the marquee, retaking the wedding photographs if lost or damaged, refund of video fees if the video is lost or damaged, public liability, etc. Study the small print carefully and make sure you are paying for what you want, and not paying for what you don't want.

Crucial Decisions

DATE (APPROXIMATE)	
DATES TO AVOID	
STYLE OF CEREMONY (CHURCH, CIVIL, ETC.)	
STYLE OF RECEPTION (FORMAL, FAMILY PARTY, ETC.)	
SIZE OF GUEST LIST	
STYLE OF HONEYMOON	
DURATION OF HONEYMOON	
OVERALL BUDGET	£
CONTRIBUTORS TO BUDGET	
BRIDE AND GROOM	£
BRIDE'S PARENTS	£
GROOM'S PARENTS	£
OTHERS	£
OTHER CONTRIBUTORS (MAKING CAKE, ETC.)	

the planning

18

The Wedding Party

BRIDE'S PARENTS:

NAMES

ADDRESS

TELEPHONE

GROOM'S PARENTS:

NAMES

ADDRESS

TELEPHONE

BEST MAN:

NAME

ADDRESS

TELEPHONE

CHIEF BRIDESMAID:

NAME

ADDRESS

TELEPHONE

BRIDESMAID 1:

NAME

ADDRESS

TELEPHONE

BRIDESMAID 2:

NAME

ADDRESS

TELEPHONE

BRIDESMAID 3:

NAME

ADDRESS

TELEPHONE

the planning

PAGE BOY 1:

NAME

ADDRESS

TELEPHONE

PAGE BOY 2:

NAME

ADDRESS

TELEPHONE

USHER 1:

NAME

ADDRESS

TELEPHONE

USHER 2:

NAME

ADDRESS

TELEPHONE

USHER 3:

NAME

ADDRESS

TELEPHONE

It is absolutely essential that you create a detailed budget plan for your wedding, keep referring to it as you go along and make sure that you are getting what you want at the price you want to pay. If you overspend, you risk either losing the service altogether – if you do not pay on time, a supplier could withdraw – or creating debts which you have to pay off later, or allowing others to get into debt. Remaining within a budget is a straightforward task if you keep a record of all your planned and actual expenditure. You can use the budget pages in this book, or even prepare your own spreadsheet on your PC so that you don't have to go over the sums.

Who Pays the Bills?

This is a checklist of who is traditionally responsible for paying for various aspects of the wedding; it may not necessarily apply to you. These days, both sets of parents usually contribute, and the bride and groom often either pay for the wedding or share the costs. You may have relations or friends – grandparents or godparents, perhaps – who would like to pay for something or contribute in another way. If you have an aunt or godmother, for example, who loves to bake and ice cakes, she will probably be delighted if you ask her to make your cake. You should always offer to pay for the ingredients – or whatever is appropriate – in such cases, but it is quite likely that 'cake' could come off your budget list altogether.

    The important point about payment responsibilities is that they are made clear from the outset. If people make different assumptions about who is responsible for the bill, it can cause awkwardness at the very least, or even real financial problems at worst. Don't fall out over money for the lack of a conversation. Discuss the circumstances at your planning meeting with both sets of parents, set your budget and agree to stick to it, decide who will be paying for what and you will be well on the way to a financially problem-free wedding. Once decisions have been made, fill in the personal allocation list to suit your own arrangements.

the finances

The Bride Traditionally Pays for

✧ The groom's ring and a gift for the groom.
✧ The hen night, although nowadays guests usually contribute.
✧ All personal items, such as hairdressing and make-up.

The Groom Traditionally Pays for

✧ The bride's ring and a gift for the bride.
✧ His own clothes and the best man's outfit.
✧ All church or register office expenses.
✧ Bouquets for the bride and bridesmaids and buttonholes and corsages for the wedding party.
✧ The stag night, although nowadays guests usually contribute.
✧ Gifts for the best man, ushers, bridesmaids and page boys.
✧ All personal items, such as a haircut.
✧ Transport for himself and the best man to the ceremony and for the bride and groom to the reception. Transport for going away and decorations for the car.
✧ The honeymoon, including insurance and inoculations.

The Bride's Parents Traditionally Pay for

✧ The bride's wedding outfit.
✧ The bride's going-away outfit.
✧ Outfits for the bridesmaids and page boys if they are not suitable for wearing again. Sometimes the bridesmaids pay for their own dresses.
✧ The press announcements.
✧ All the wedding stationery.
✧ The photographer and videographer.
✧ Flowers for the ceremony and reception.
✧ Wedding transport.
✧ The reception and catering.
✧ The wedding cake.

Cost Allocation Sheet

ITEM	PERSON RESPONSIBLE
BRIDE'S OUTFIT	
BRIDESMAIDS' OUTFITS	
PAGE BOYS' OUTFITS	
GROOM'S OUTFIT	
BEST MAN'S OUTFIT	
BRIDE'S BOUQUET	
BRIDESMAIDS' BOUQUETS	
BUTTONHOLES AND CORSAGES	
FLOWERS FOR THE CEREMONY VENUE	
FLOWERS FOR THE RECEPTION VENUE	
BRIDE'S RING	
GROOM'S RING	
GIFTS FOR THE BRIDESMAIDS AND PAGE BOYS	
GIFTS FOR THE BEST MAN AND USHERS	
TRANSPORT TO THE CHURCH FOR THE GROOM AND THE BEST MAN	
TRANSPORT TO THE CHURCH FOR THE BRIDE, BRIDE'S FATHER AND BRIDESMAIDS	
TRANSPORT TO THE RECEPTION FOR THE BRIDE AND GROOM	
PRESS ANNOUNCEMENTS	
WEDDING STATIONERY	
PHOTOGRAPHER	
VIDEOGRAPHER	
CHURCH/REGISTER OFFICE EXPENSES	
RECEPTION VENUE	
RECEPTION CATERING	
RECEPTION DRINKS	
MUSICIANS/ENTERTAINERS	
WEDDING CAKE	
HEN NIGHT	
STAG NIGHT	
BRIDE'S GOING-AWAY OUTFIT	
HONEYMOON	

the finances

Setting the Budget

You have an overall figure in mind and lots of information on the costs of various supplies and services. Personalise these budget sheets to suit your own needs and use them to keep a record of all your financial planning information. Use the quick-reference sheet for overall figures, so that you have a complete picture at a glance, and fill in the full details on the other pages.

- ✧ Go through each item in turn and obtain estimates or quotations. Write them into your budget sheet.
- ✧ Remember that an estimate is just that, whereas a quotation is a fixed price, although it will probably have a specified time limit.
- ✧ Deal with reputable companies and check references if appropriate.
- ✧ If everything adds up to the budget figure, go ahead. If not, make adjustments and look on pages 169–72 for some potential money-saving tips. Remember what really matters to you and compromise everywhere else. If nothing will do but being driven to and from the church in a coach and four, then compromise on the dress, the wine, the honeymoon – anything but that!
- ✧ Once you are sure that you are happy with a particular supplier, check any contracts and confirm all bookings and details in writing to make sure your booking is guaranteed.
- ✧ Pay deposits on time to secure your bookings.
- ✧ Check that public liability and cancellations insurances are available.
- ✧ Allow yourself a margin of 5–10 per cent.

the finances

Quick-reference Budget Sheet

ITEM	ESTIMATES	QUOTATION
CEREMONY VENUE		
RECEPTION VENUE		
CATERING		
DRINKS		
THE CAKE		
MUSICIANS/ENTERTAINMENT		
BRIDE'S OUTFIT		
BEAUTY TREATMENTS		
BRIDESMAIDS' AND ATTENDANTS' OUTFITS		
MENSWEAR		
FLOWERS		
RINGS		
GIFTS		
PRESS ANNOUNCEMENTS		
STATIONERY		
PHOTOGRAPHS		
VIDEO		
TRANSPORT		
HONEYMOON		
TOTAL:		

the finances

Budget Breakdown

COST CENTRE	QUOTATION	DEPOSIT
CEREMONY VENUE:		
CHURCH/REGISTER OFFICE FEES		
FEE FOR MINISTER/REGISTRAR		
BANNS		
LICENCE OR CERTIFICATE		
BELLS		
CHOIR		
FLOWERS		
MUSIC		
PERSONAL DONATION		
RECEPTION VENUE:		
HIRE OF ROOMS		
DECORATIONS		
FURNITURE		
FOOD AND DRINK:		
FOOD		
HIRE OF EQUIPMENT		
SERVERS		
DRINKS WITH MEAL		
DRINKS WITH TOASTS		
OTHER DRINKS		
BAR ATTENDANT		
HIRE OF GLASSWARE		
WEDDING CAKE		
ENTERTAINMENT:		
MUSICIANS OR DJ		
BRIDE'S OUTFITS:		
DRESS		
HEADDRESS		
TRAIN		
SHOES		
UNDERWEAR		
HOSIERY		

the finances

DEPOSIT PAID	BALANCE	BALANCE DUE	BALANCE PAID

the finances

COST CENTRE	QUOTATION	DEPOSIT
JEWELLERY		
GOING-AWAY OUTFIT AND SHOES		
BEAUTY TREATMENTS:		
HAIRDRESSER		
MAKE-UP ARTIST		
BEAUTICIAN		
PERFUME		
GROOM'S HAIRDRESSER		
BRIDESMAIDS'/PAGEBOYS' OUTFITS:		
CHIEF BRIDESMAID'S DRESS		
BRIDESMAID'S DRESS 1		
BRIDESMAID'S DRESS 2		
BRIDESMAID'S DRESS 3		
CHIEF BRIDESMAID'S HEADDRESS		
BRIDESMAID'S HEADDRESS 1		
BRIDESMAID'S HEADDRESS 2		
BRIDESMAID'S HEADDRESS 3		
CHIEF BRIDESMAID'S SHOES		
BRIDESMAID'S SHOES 1		
BRIDESMAID'S SHOES 2		
BRIDESMAID'S SHOES 3		
CHIEF BRIDESMAID'S HOSIERY ETC.		
BRIDESMAID'S HOSIERY ETC. 1		
BRIDESMAID'S HOSIERY ETC. 2		
BRIDESMAID'S HOSIERY ETC. 3		
PAGE BOY'S OUTFIT 1		
PAGE BOY'S OUTFIT 2		
MENSWEAR:		
GROOM'S SUIT		
GROOM'S SHIRT, SHOES, ETC.		
BEST MAN'S SUIT		
BEST MAN'S SHIRT, SHOES, ETC.		
USHER'S SUIT 1		
USHER'S SHIRT, SHOES ETC. 1		
USHER'S SUIT 2		
USHER'S SHIRT, SHOES ETC. 2		

DEPOSIT PAID	BALANCE	BALANCE DUE	BALANCE PAID

the finances

COST CENTRE	QUOTATION	DEPOSIT
FLOWERS:		
BRIDE'S BOUQUET		
CHIEF BRIDESMAID'S BOUQUET		
BRIDESMAID'S BOUQUET 1		
BRIDESMAID'S BOUQUET 2		
BRIDESMAID'S BOUQUET 3		
BUTTONHOLES		
BRIDE'S MOTHER'S CORSAGE		
GROOM'S MOTHER'S CORSAGE		
CHURCH FLOWERS		
RECEPTION FLOWERS		
RINGS:		
BRIDE'S RING		
GROOM'S RING		
GIFTS:		
FOR THE BRIDE		
FOR THE GROOM		
FOR THE BRIDESMAIDS		
FOR THE PAGE BOYS		
FOR THE BEST MAN		
FOR THE BRIDE'S PARENTS		
FOR THE GROOM'S PARENTS		
FOR THE USHERS		
PRESS ANNOUNCEMENTS:		
BEFORE THE WEDDING		
AFTER THE WEDDING		
STATIONERY:		
INVITATIONS AND ENVELOPES		
MAPS		
POSTAGE FOR INVITATIONS		
ORDER OF SERVICE SHEETS		
MENUS		
PLACE CARDS		
CAKE BOXES		
POSTAGE FOR CAKE		

DEPOSIT PAID	BALANCE	BALANCE DUE	BALANCE PAID

the finances

COST CENTRE	QUOTATION	DEPOSIT
STATIONERY:		
FOR THANK-YOU LETTERS		
POSTAGE FOR THANK-YOU LETTERS		
KEEPSAKE ALBUM		
GUEST BOOK		
PHOTOGRAPHS:		
PACKAGE FOR BRIDE AND GROOM		
PACKAGE FOR BRIDE'S PARENTS		
PACKAGE FOR GROOM'S PARENTS		
COST OF PRINTS		
VIDEO:		
COST OF SERVICE		
COST OF COPIES		
TRANSPORT:		
BRIDE AND FATHER TO CEREMONY		
BRIDE'S MOTHER AND BRIDESMAIDS TO CEREMONY		
GROOM & BEST MAN TO CEREMONY		
BRIDE AND GROOM TO RECEPTION		
PARENTS TO RECEPTION		
BEST MAN TO RECEPTION		
BRIDE & GROOM FROM RECEPTION		
DECORATIONS FOR CARS		
HONEYMOON:		
FIRST-NIGHT ACCOMMODATION		
TRAVEL		
ACCOMMODATION		
INSURANCE		
CLOTHES		
LUGGAGE		
DOCUMENTS		
INOCULATIONS		
SPENDING MONEY		

DEPOSIT PAID	BALANCE	BALANCE DUE	BALANCE PAID

the finances

The exact timescale of your planning will obviously depend on how far in advance you have set your wedding. Advantages of giving yourself plenty of time are that you will get the best choice of services if you book early; you may be able to benefit from sales and discounts; you can spread the costs; and the whole thing will be less rushed so you will not feel forced into making quick decisions before you have had time to consider the options fully.

This outline is based on having six months to do all the planning and preparation. If you are starting earlier, or indeed later, you can easily adjust the section headings to suit your own circumstances. In any event, you will want to make your own changes to the list as you work through. Some of the items will be on-going – for example, writing thank-you letters for gifts received – so unless you are sure you have ticked off a job as completely finished, it may be a good idea to run your eye down the whole list from time to time.

If you do have more than six months to plan your wedding, do start your planning straight away so you can use the time wisely. You will probably find that you can make quite a few bookings early, then take loads of leisurely time thinking and planning, before you commit yourselves to specific arrangements or suppliers.

Since popular church and reception venues do tend to be booked up well in advance, especially for summer weddings, book these as soon as you have confirmed both the date and style of your wedding with those closest to you. Select and invite your wedding party as well so they don't book their annual holiday to clash with the wedding day.

Once you have sorted out those main items, start to look around at services, send away for catalogues and information and read wedding magazines so that you have a firm idea of the range of suppliers and services available. You may find new ideas that would never have occurred to you otherwise.

Keep an up-to-date record of what you have and have not done, and as soon as you are sure you have found exactly what you are looking for, book it immediately to be sure your ideal services are secured.

the timing

If you are moving into a new home together, then you should also begin house-hunting as soon as possible, particularly if you are planning to buy rather than rent. House-buying is a notoriously difficult process, fraught with all kinds of legal problems and delays and, whether you are renting or buying, just finding the right home can take up a great deal of time. By making an early start, you give yourselves the best chance of finding exactly what you want and of avoiding the horrors of a last-minute hitch, such as being gazumped a week before the wedding.

The first thing to do when you start your wedding plans, of course, is to set the date, and there are quite a few things to consider before you make your final decision.

◇ Do you particularly want a spring, summer, autumn or winter wedding?
◇ How much time do you want to spend in the planning stages?
◇ Will all your wedding party be available?
◇ Are there any work commitments to take into consideration?
◇ Do you have any business travel planned which you could use to your advantage?
◇ How much time do you need to save up?
◇ Will you time your wedding to coincide with your two-week annual holiday?
◇ Are you hoping to take advantage of off-season honeymoon discounts?
◇ Is the traditional Saturday the best day for you, or would you consider a weekday ceremony? If so, will your guests be able to attend?
◇ Are you inviting any special guests – perhaps from abroad – whose needs must be considered?
◇ What about overnight accommodation for guests? Can this be arranged in good time?
◇ If you are having a dress made, do you have enough time?

Use the space on the following pages to make your own schedule notes.

the timing

The Planning

✧ Discuss plans with the family.
✧ Choose the type of ceremony.
✧ Choose the type of reception.
✧ Set the budget.
✧ Think about the style of catering.
✧ Think about the arrangements for drinks.
✧ Think about the style of flowers.
✧ Think about wedding transport
✧ Discuss the honeymoon.

The Ceremony

✧ Choose the ceremony venue, date and time.
✧ Book the ceremony.
✧ Arrange the banns or licence.

The Wedding Party and Guests

✧ Choose the attendants.
✧ Compile a wedding guest list.

The Reception

✧ Choose the reception venue, date and time.
✧ Book the reception venue.
✧ Choose and book the caterer.
✧ Choose and book the drinks supplier.
✧ Arrange for catering equipment hire.
✧ Choose and book musicians or a disco.

Other Arrangements

✧ Choose and book the photographer.
✧ Choose and book the videographer.
✧ Choose and book the florist.
✧ Choose and book the transport.
✧ Choose and book the honeymoon.
✧ Book time off work.
✧ Look for somewhere to live.

the timing

Five Months Before

The Planning

✧ Review the budget.
✧ Review the schedule.
✧ Have you forgotten anything?

The Clothes

✧ Choose your wedding dress.
✧ Buy underwear, shoes and accessories.
✧ Choose the bridesmaids' dresses and page boys' outfits.
✧ Book the hire firm for formal wear and arrange fittings.

The Reception

✧ Finalise the menu.

Other Arrangements

✧ Arrange wedding insurance cover.
✧ Prepare a wedding gift list.

the timing

Four Months Before

The Planning

✧ Review the budget.
✧ Review the schedule.
✧ Have you forgotten anything?

The Ceremony

✧ Select the music and hymns for the ceremony.
✧ Organise the choir and bell-ringing.
✧ Finalise the order of service.

Other Arrangements

✧ Choose and order the stationery.
✧ Order or bake the cake.
✧ Select the bouquets, corsages and buttonholes.
✧ Finalise the flowers or decorations for the ceremony and reception venues.
✧ Buy the rings.

the timing

The Planning

✧ Review the budget.
✧ Review the schedule.
✧ Have you forgotten anything?

The Ceremony

✧ Book the registrar or confirm civil arrangements.

The Honeymoon

✧ Apply for a new passport if you are changing your name (see pages 161–2).
✧ Arrange visas or travel documents.
✧ Arrange inoculations.
✧ Visit the family planning clinic.
✧ Arrange going-away and honeymoon clothes.

Other Arrangements

✧ Finalise the photograph arrangements.
✧ Finalise the video arrangements.
✧ Check arrangements for new home.

the timing

Two Months Before

The Planning

✦ Review the budget.
✦ Review the schedule.
✦ Have you forgotten anything?

The Guests

✦ Collect the stationery and send out invitations (at least six weeks in advance).
✦ Record acceptances and refusals.
✦ Place the wedding gift list with a local store.
✦ Record gifts received and write thank-you letters.
✦ Choose and wrap gifts for the groom, attendants and parents.

The Reception

✦ Begin preparing and freezing food if self-catering.
✦ Order or buy drinks for reception if supplying your own.

Other Arrangements

✦ Buy ribbons for wedding cars.
✦ Book accommodation for the wedding night.

the timing

the timing

The Planning

✧ Review the budget.
✧ Review the schedule.
✧ Have you forgotten anything?

Confirm Arrangements

✧ Ceremony venue ❑
✧ Reception venue ❑
✧ Caterers ❑
✧ Drinks supplier ❑
✧ Musicians or disco ❑
✧ Photographer ❑
✧ Videographer ❑
✧ Florist ❑
✧ Dressmaker ❑
✧ Outfitters ❑
✧ Cake-maker ❑
✧ Travel agent ❑

The Clothes

✧ Arrange final dressing fittings and delivery.
✧ Try on dress with all underwear, shoes and accessories.
✧ 'Wear in' wedding shoes.

The Honeymoon

✧ Order travellers' cheques and foreign currency.

Other Arrangements

✧ Buy cake boxes.
✧ Visit the hairdresser with your headdress and veil to decide on styles.
✧ Practise make-up.
✧ Arrange hen and stag nights.
✧ Arrange transport and hospitality for attendants.
✧ Arrange press announcements.
✧ Make arrangements for dressing and preparations on the morning of the wedding.

Three Weeks Before

The Planning

✧ Review the budget.
✧ Review the schedule.
✧ Have you forgotten anything?

The Ceremony

✧ Attend church for the reading of the banns.

The Reception

✧ Prepare seating plan and write place cards.

Other Arrangements

✧ Send out change of name/address information (see page 162).
✧ Continue preparations for moving into new home.

the timing

Two Weeks Before

The Planning

✧ Review the budget.
✧ Review the schedule.
✧ Have you forgotten anything?

The Reception

✧ Confirm the final number of guests with the caterer.
✧ Ice the cake or take delivery.
✧ Prepare speeches.

Other Arrangements

✧ Arrange a display of the gifts either at the bride's home or another suitable venue (see pages 78–9).
✧ Have the going-away car serviced.

the timing

One Week Before

The Planning

✧ Have you forgotten anything?

The Ceremony

✧ Attend rehearsal.
✧ Make sure the attendants know their duties.
✧ Double-check that the best man will pick up buttonholes and order of service sheets.
✧ Collect certificates/licences etc.

The Honeymoon

✧ Pack clothes and documents.

Other Arrangements

✧ Plan the wedding-day timetable.
✧ Check whether any (other) special events might cause traffic delays on the day.
✧ Enjoy the hen or stag night.
✧ Appoint someone to take care of the wedding gifts after the wedding.
✧ Check the arrangements for the return of hired clothes.
✧ Make sure announcements will be sent to the press.

the timing

A Few Days Before

The Clothes

✧ Collect hired items.

The Reception

✧ Prepare food for reception if self-catering.
✧ Finalise drinks arrangements if self-catering.
✧ Collect hired glassware or catering equipment.

The Honeymoon

✧ Arrange for honeymoon luggage and clothes to be taken to reception venue.
✧ Collect travellers' cheques and foreign currency.

That covers the planning before the event. If you want to do a full run-through and read the order of events on the wedding day itself, turn to page 153. Otherwise, I think it would be a good idea to take a breath and go back to the beginning.

the timing

Who cares who does what as long as it gets done?! That's the key to this section, which outlines the people who are traditionally responsible for the various tasks. The importance of this information is to make sure that someone – whoever that may be – knows they are responsible for a particular job and will go ahead and do it. If you make assumptions, you are likely to run into trouble, but if you check and confirm exactly what you expect of your planning and organising team, then no one will be left saying, 'But I thought you were going to pick up the groom's suit!'

Look through the list, think about those who are helping you and personalise the information, then you can run through each set of duties with your mum, the best man, the chief bridesmaid and so on, to make sure that they are happy with what is expected of them. They will almost certainly feel relieved that you have taken the initiative and made everything crystal clear.

Making Your Plans

There are four clear stages to the planning and organisation of the wedding, and each person involved will have a different set of things to do, depending on their particular role. Some – like the bride and her mother – will have a lot more to do before the event, while others – like the bridesmaids and ushers – are mainly involved on the big day itself. Bear in mind how busy people are when you are allocating jobs. If you know, for example, that the best man will be travelling on business in the run-up to the wedding, try to assign some of his tasks to the groom, your father or one of the ushers.

who does what?

The Bride

The bride, assisted by her mother, is the one likely to be doing most of the decision-making and organising for any wedding. However, even though many of the decisions may not traditionally involve the groom, good communication with him is essential if the planning and preparations are to go smoothly.

Before the Event

- ◇ Help to set the budget and agree the financial responsibilities for the wedding with the groom and both sets of parents.
- ◇ Draw up the guest list with her mother and the groom's parents.
- ◇ Choose attendants with the groom.
- ◇ Decide on the ceremony venue, date and time with the groom.
- ◇ Select hymns and service details with the groom.
- ◇ Attend church with the groom for the reading of the banns.
- ◇ Arrange the reception and catering with her mother.
- ◇ Order the wedding cake with her mother.
- ◇ Arrange musicians or DJ with her mother.
- ◇ Choose and buy her dress and accessories.
- ◇ Organise the bridesmaids' dresses with her mother.
- ◇ Organise the flowers with her mother.
- ◇ Choose and order the stationery with her mother.
- ◇ Arrange transport with her mother.
- ◇ Choose and book a photographer with her mother.
- ◇ Choose and book the honeymoon with the groom.
- ◇ Organise passport/visa/inoculations/foreign currency with the groom.
- ◇ Look for somewhere to live – with the groom!
- ◇ Compile the wedding gift list with the groom and place it with a store, if appropriate.
- ◇ Record gifts received and write thank-you letters.
- ◇ Buy gifts for the groom and attendants.
- ◇ Buy the rings with the groom.
- ◇ Send out change of name/address information (see pages 161–2).
- ◇ Enjoy the hen night.

On the Day

✧ Be the last to arrive at the church with her father and stay centre stage for the ceremony, recessional and photographs.

At the Reception

✧ Leave first for the reception but arrive second, after the bride's parents, and join the receiving line to welcome guests.
✧ Begin the meal first.
✧ Cut the cake with the groom.
✧ Dance the first dance with the groom and then her father.
✧ Dance with the male members of the wedding party and family.
✧ Have a wonderful day!
✧ Thank everyone for their contribution.
✧ Throw the bouquet, leave for the honeymoon and let everyone else clear up.

After the Event

✧ Write thank-you letters
✧ Make a new will.
✧ Alter existing insurance policies to new name and beneficiary.
✧ Take out new insurance policies if required.
✧ Entertain the principal members of the wedding party with the groom.

who does what?

The Groom

Some grooms have a lot to do with the decision-making and organisation of a wedding; others sit back and leave it to the bride and her mother. However, it is vital that the groom makes his preferences known and acts in a supportive role even if he may not be taking a very active part in the planning.

Before the Event

- ✧ Help to set the budget and agree the financial responsibilities for the wedding with the bride and both sets of parents.
- ✧ Choose attendants with the bride.
- ✧ Decide on the ceremony venue, date and time with the bride.
- ✧ Select hymns and service details with the bride.
- ✧ Make appropriate payments for the ceremony.
- ✧ Attend church with the bride for the reading of the banns.
- ✧ Choose and book the honeymoon with the bride.
- ✧ Organise passport/visa/inoculations/foreign currency with the bride.
- ✧ Look for somewhere to live – with the bride!
- ✧ Compile the wedding gift list with the bride.
- ✧ Buy the rings with the bride.
- ✧ Buy gifts for the bride and attendants.
- ✧ Arrange for hire or purchase of suit, shoes and accessories.
- ✧ Buy ribbons for the wedding cars.
- ✧ Write a speech.
- ✧ Check over duties with the best man.
- ✧ Enjoy the stag night.

On the Day

- ✧ Arrive in good time at the church and stay centre stage for the ceremony, recessional and photographs.

who does what?

At the Reception

✦ Leave first for the reception but arrive second, after the bride's parents, and join the receiving line to welcome guests.
✦ Begin the meal first.
✦ Cut the cake with the bride.
✦ Make a speech.
✦ Dance the first dance with the bride and then the bride's mother.
✦ Dance with the female members of the wedding party and family.
✦ Have a wonderful day!
✦ Thank everyone for their contribution.
✦ Leave for the honeymoon and let everyone else clear up.

After the Event

✦ Write thank-you letters
✦ Make a new will.
✦ Alter existing insurance policies to new beneficiary.
✦ Take out new insurance policies if required.
✦ Entertain the principal members of the wedding party with the bride.

The Bride's Mother

Although definitely in a supporting role on the actual day, the bride's mother is usually the one who, with the bride, does most of the hard work before the event, making sure everything is well organised.

Before the Event

✦ Help to set the budget and agree the financial responsibilities for the wedding with the bride and groom and the groom's parents.
✦ Buy a wedding outfit. Discuss colours with the groom's mother.
✦ Draw up the guest list with the bride and the groom's parents.
✦ Arrange press announcements.
✦ Choose and order the stationery with the bride.
✦ Send out invitations and list replies.

- ✧ Arrange the reception and catering with the bride.
- ✧ Arrange the seating plan for the reception.
- ✧ Order the wedding cake with the bride.
- ✧ Arrange musicians or DJ with the bride.
- ✧ Organise the bridesmaids' dresses with the bride.
- ✧ Organise the flowers with the bride.
- ✧ Arrange transport with the bride.
- ✧ Choose and book a photographer with the bride.
- ✧ Organise the wedding-present display.
- ✧ Arrange any overnight accommodation required.

On the Day

- ✧ Make sure the best man has the buttonholes and order of service sheets.
- ✧ Help the bride to arrange her veil.
- ✧ Be the last to be seated at the church, escorted by the chief usher, before the arrival of the wedding party.
- ✧ Join the wedding party for the signing of the register.
- ✧ Be escorted from the church by the groom's father.
- ✧ Be ready for all the photographs.
- ✧ Leave for the reception with the groom's father.

At the Reception

- ✧ Be the first to arrive at the reception and head the receiving line with the bride's father.
- ✧ Act as hostess for the occasion.
- ✧ Check the gift display, if appropriate.
- ✧ Take charge of the wedding gifts and the cake.

After the Event

- ✧ Send cake to anyone who was not able to attend the wedding.
- ✧ Organise the distribution of the photograph proofs and the collection of the orders.

The Bride's Father

The bride's father traditionally 'gives away' the bride – a relic of the times when she was a chattel to be passed from one male to another! Traditionally, he also footed the bill – fortunately for him, another custom which has undergone some changes in recent years.

Before the Event

✧ Help to set the budget and agree the financial responsibilities for the wedding with the bride and groom and the groom's parents.
✧ Buy or hire a wedding suit.
✧ Write a speech.
✧ Pay the bills.

On the Day

✧ Leave home with the bride.
✧ Escort the bride down the aisle on his right arm. Take a step back and remain at the chancel steps for the ceremony.
✧ Join the wedding party for the signing of the register.
✧ Escort the groom's mother out of the church.
✧ Be available for the photographs.
✧ Leave for the reception with the groom's mother.

At the Reception

✧ Arrive first at the reception and head the receiving line with the bride's mother.
✧ Ask the minister to say 'Grace', or do so.
✧ Indicate to the waitresses to start serving.
✧ Make a speech to propose the toast to the bride and groom.
✧ Interrupt the first dance to dance with the bride.
✧ Act as host for the occasion.

After the Event

✧ Return suit if hired.
✧ Pay the bills.

who does what?

The Groom's Parents

The involvement of the groom's parents will vary tremendously depending on your own circumstances since, traditionally, the bride's parents did all the hard work and paid all the bills. Now, this has changed considerably, but if the groom's parents want to be involved – in practical and/or financial ways – it is helpful if they make the first move and offer their support so that the bride's parents do not feel they are either asking too much or missing opportunities of including the groom's parents in the planning and responsibilities involved. Once the subject has been broached, everyone will feel much more able to discuss the options.

Before the Event

✦ Help to set the budget and agree the financial responsibilities for the wedding with the bride and groom and the bride's parents.
✦ Help to prepare the guest list with the bride and her mother.
✦ Contribute in any other ways agreed with the couple and their families.

On the Day

✦ Arrive at the church in good time and sit behind the groom and best man.
✦ Join the wedding party at the signing of the register.
✦ Join the recessional and be involved in the photographs.
✦ Leave after the bride and groom with the bride's parents.

At the Reception

✦ Arrive at the reception after the bride and groom and the bride's parents and join the receiving line.
✦ Help the party to go smoothly by dancing with guests and making introductions.

... who does what?

After the Event

✧ Write thank-you letters to the bride's parents for arranging the wedding.
✧ Write thank-you letters to the bride and groom if presents have been received.

The Best Man

It is important to make clear what you expect of your best man at the wedding, as the amount of responsibility he takes for the smooth running of the event does vary considerably.

Before the Event

✧ Time the journeys between groom's home and ceremony venue.
✧ Arrange for hire or purchase of his suit, shoes and accessories.
✧ Make sure the ushers know their duties.
✧ Clean the car and tie on ribbons.
✧ Prepare a speech.
✧ Arrange the stag night for the groom, ushers and close friends – including safe transport home. Invite the bride's and groom's fathers (although they usually leave early). In the past, the groom often paid for the stag night, but nowadays the guests are more likely to contribute; make sure everyone is clear about this.

On the Day

✧ Make sure he has the rings.
✧ Collect the buttonholes and order of service sheets from the bride's mother.
✧ Get the groom to the church on time.
✧ Give order of service sheets to the minister for the wedding party.
✧ Give the buttonholes to the ushers for distribution.
✧ Take a seat at the front of the church with the groom and support him during the ceremony.
✧ Join the wedding party for the signing of the register.
✧ Escort the chief bridesmaid from the church in the recessional.

who does what?

- ✧ Join in the photographs and help to organise guests if required.
- ✧ Escort the bride and groom to their car.
- ✧ Escort the parents to their cars.
- ✧ Make sure the chief usher takes over to get everyone safely to the reception.
- ✧ Leave for the reception.

At the Reception

- ✧ Join the receiving line to welcome guests.
- ✧ Act as toastmaster.
- ✧ Make a speech.
- ✧ Dance the second dance with the chief bridesmaid, and dance with as many of the female wedding guests as possible.
- ✧ Help to make the party run smoothly.
- ✧ Check that nothing has been left behind by the male guests.

After the Event

- ✧ Write thank-you letter.
- ✧ Arrange for return of hired suits.

The Chief Bridesmaid

Friendship and support are the main contributions of the chief bridesmaid. The closer she is to the bride – both in relationship and location – the greater the degree of input she will have in the planning.

Before the Event

- ✧ Help with decisions on dresses and outfits if required.
- ✧ Provide any support needed by the bride.
- ✧ Make sure the bridesmaids know their duties.
- ✧ Arrange the hen night.

On the Day

- ✧ Arrive at the bride's house on the morning of the wedding to dress, put on make-up, if appropriate, and arrange hair.
- ✧ Leave before the bride and arrive at the church.
- ✧ Follow the bride down the aisle, lift her veil and look after her bouquet at the chancel steps.
- ✧ Join the wedding party for the signing of the register.
- ✧ Be escorted from the church by the best man after the ceremony.
- ✧ Be in the right place at the right time for the photographs.
- ✧ Leave for the reception after the couple's parents.

At the Reception

- ✧ Join the receiving line to welcome guests.
- ✧ Ask guests to sign the keepsake book.
- ✧ Dance the second dance with the best man.
- ✧ Dance with guests and generally help to keep the party going smoothly.
- ✧ Help the bride to change into her going-away outfit.
- ✧ Check that nothing has been left behind by the female guests.

After the Event

- ✧ Write thank-you letter.
- ✧ Arrange for return of any hired items.

who does what?

The Bridesmaids and Page Boys

Bridesmaids are unmarried girls; married attendants are called 'matrons of honour'. They are usually sisters, relatives or close friends of the bride and are there to support the bride and look decorative on the day.

Before the Event

❖ If the bridesmaids are buying their own dresses, consult with the bride and agree a suitable style. If the bride is paying for the outfits, she will have the choice of style.

❖ Buy or have the dress and accessories made.

On the Day

❖ Arrive at the bride's house on the morning of the wedding to dress, put on make-up, if appropriate, and arrange hair.

❖ Leave before the bride and arrive at the church.

❖ Follow the bride down the aisle and wait at the chancel steps or sit during the service, as instructed.

❖ If there is a flower girl, she should walk in front of the bride spreading flower petals on the ground.

❖ Follow the chief bridesmaid and best man out of the church after the ceremony.

❖ If there is a ring-bearer, he should hold the rings on a satin cushion to give to the best man at the appropriate point in the ceremony.

❖ Be in the right place at the right time for the photographs.

❖ Leave for the reception after the couple's parents.

At the Reception

❖ Younger bridesmaids will simply enjoy the party, but may like to help distribute slices of cake.

❖ Older bridesmaids can help by introducing guests to each other, dancing with guests, helping to serve drinks or assisting older or younger guests.

❖ Help to decorate the bride and groom's going-away car.

who does what?

After the Event

✧ Return the outfit if it has been hired.
✧ Write a thank-you letter to the bride and groom for their gift.

The Ushers

Traditionally there are as many ushers as bridesmaids, as one of their duties is to escort the ladies throughout the day. Since this is no longer necessary, the groom usually asks his brothers or a few close friends to act as ushers (one usher to every fifty guests is a good rule of thumb but it doesn't really matter). Their role is generally to look after the bridesmaids and to assist the best man and groom in making the day run smoothly.

Before the Event

✧ Appoint a chief usher.
✧ Attend the stag night (that'll be hard work).
✧ For a formal wedding, find out the dress code and arrange to hire a suit and all necessary accessories.
✧ For an informal wedding, buy (or have cleaned and ready) a lounge suit, shirt, tie and shoes.
✧ Buy or borrow an umbrella to shelter guests if it rains.
✧ Double-check the arrival time at the church or ceremony venue.
✧ Find out whether photography is allowed in the church.
✧ If either set of parents is divorced, make sure of the bride's preferred seating arrangements.
✧ Clean the car if driving guests to the reception.

On the Day

✧ Arrive first at the church or ceremony venue at the agreed time.
✧ Obtain their buttonholes and the order of service sheets from the best man.
✧ Give sufficient order of service sheets to the minister for the wedding party.
✧ Help with the parking arrangements.
✧ Reserve the front pews for the parents of the bride and groom.

who does what?

- ◆ Welcome guests at the church and hand them order of service sheets.
- ◆ Tactfully mention, if necessary, that photography is not allowed in the church.
- ◆ Show them to seats on the left, if they are family or friends of the bride, and seats on the right, if they are family or friends of the groom.
- ◆ Seat immediate family behind the parents of the bride or groom.
- ◆ Escort single ladies to their seats.
- ◆ When the wedding party arrive at the church, the chief usher escorts the bride's mother to her seat, then all the ushers take their seats at the back of the church.
- ◆ Direct the guests to the area where the photographs are to be taken and assist while the photographer is working.
- ◆ After the best man has left for the reception in order to join the receiving line, the chief usher takes charge of making sure everyone has transport to the reception.
- ◆ The chief usher makes sure nothing has been left behind in the church.
- ◆ The ushers are last to leave for the reception.

At the Reception

- ◆ Offer drinks to guests on arrival.
- ◆ Help with the smooth running of the event by introducing guests to each other, dancing with guests, helping to serve drinks and helping with elderly guests or children.
- ◆ Decorate the bride and groom's going-away car.
- ◆ After the party, offer help to make sure everyone is taken home safely and nothing is left behind.

If you and the groom are committed followers of a particular faith, then obviously you will want to be married in your local church, synagogue or place of worship and will already be familiar with the minister.

If you are from different faiths, then the first thing to do is to discuss with the ministers of both your churches how to combine the service in an appropriate way. For example, you may wish to be married in a Church of England ceremony with a Roman Catholic priest in attendance to give his blessing.

- ✧ If you do want a religious ceremony, you must contact the minister at the church to discuss the implications of your choice.
- ✧ The minister will certainly expect you to attend pre-wedding discussions about the significance of the service. If you are not regular members of the congregation, you are likely to be asked to attend, or the minister may decline to marry you in the church.
- ✧ There are residency requirements for church weddings; check that you conform to the legal requirements (see pages 165–8).
- ✧ Any church service must be witnessed by two people over the age of 18.
- ✧ The occasion can be as formal as you wish.
- ✧ You may have as many attendants as you wish.
- ✧ The number of guests is limited only by the size of the church or premises.
- ✧ Churches may not allow flowers during Lent or Advent, or sometimes at other times of year.
- ✧ Summer dates, in particular, may be booked more than a year in advance.

the minister

Church Details

The church notice board or parish magazine will give you information on the timing of initial wedding interviews. Often the minister sets aside Saturday morning, for example, for those wishing to discuss weddings or christenings.

✧ Choose and confirm the date and time of the ceremony.

✧ Make arrangements for the banns to be read.

✧ If the groom is from a different parish, visit the minister of that parish to arrange for the banns to be read simultaneously in that parish church.

✧ Choose which of the services you wish to follow. The different services can be found in *The Book of Common Prayer 1662, The Book of Common Prayer 1928* and *The Alternative Service 1980*.

✧ Arrange subsequent meetings to go through the ceremony and discuss the significance of the words and the vows.

✧ Discuss payment and confirm the fees for the church.

✧ Decide whether you wish to include Holy Communion or Mass.

✧ Choose readings and arrange for an appropriate reader.

✧ Confirm the order of service.

✧ Discuss arrangements for bell-ringing, including costs.

✧ Discuss arrangements for the church flowers. You may be able to give a donation to the church and have them decorate the church, in which case find out whether you can discuss colour schemes with other brides who are to be married on the same day.

✧ Find out whether the minister allows photographs to be taken in the church. Often, ministers will allow perhaps three photographs at particular points in the service.

✧ Find out whether a video camera would be allowed and, if so, whether you could look round the church with the videographer and check on lighting and sound facilities.

the minister

- ❖ Find out whether confetti is allowed in the church grounds and, if so, confirm that you will ask your guests to use rice-paper confetti only.
- ❖ Check whether the minister arranges a rehearsal; not all churches do this.
- ❖ The minister can be a great source of information on all aspects of weddings, gathered from his own experience. Ask him for any suggestions or recommendations he may wish to make.
- ❖ If the bride intends to change her name and wishes to apply for a passport, she must obtain form PD2 from the Post Office and ask the minister to sign the form. If time is short, however, it is not necessary to change the passport in order to travel. The bride needs only to have her tickets and any other documentation in her maiden name, as on her passport, and simply carry her marriage certificate with her.

The Church Music

There is more information on music in on pages 105–6.

- ❖ Find out whether an organist automatically attends, whether you need to book or whether the church uses taped music. Check whether there is an additional charge for the organist.
- ❖ Choose the hymns.
- ❖ Choose the type of music to be played before the service, for the processional and recessional. Check whether these will be played by the organist or whether you will need to provide tapes and a tape recorder. You can buy cassettes of music specially designed for weddings – look in the bridal magazines and in music stores. Make sure that the pieces of music are of the right length.
- ❖ Check on the music to be played while you are signing the register. Will the congregation sing a hymn, will the choir sing or will you be entertained by a soloist or other music?
- ❖ Discuss any arrangements for a choir, including additional costs.
- ❖ If you are inviting a soloist, confirm that your choice of piece is acceptable to the minister. Check whether any special sound equipment is needed.

the minister

Later Meetings

- ✧ You should give the minister the opportunity to check the order of service sheets if he or she wishes.
- ✧ You may like to offer an invitation to the minister to attend the wedding breakfast.
- ✧ If the minister does attend, you should invite him or her to say 'Grace' before the meal.

A Service of Blessing

Some couples, perhaps if one of them has been divorced, choose to combine a civil ceremony (see next chapter) with a service of blessing.

- ✧ This follows a civil ceremony either on the same day or later.
- ✧ It can include Holy Communion or Mass, and hymns, prayers and readings, depending on the circumstances.
- ✧ It does not include an exchange of vows.
- ✧ No witnesses are required.

the minister

Church Details

CHURCH:

ADDRESS

TELEPHONE

NAME OF MINISTER

ADDRESS

TELEPHONE

DATE OF CEREMONY

TIME OF CEREMONY

DATES FOR BANNS TO BE READ

DATES FOR DISCUSSION MEETINGS

GROOM'S CHURCH:

MINISTER

ADDRESS

TELEPHONE

BANNS ORGANISED

SERVICE:

HYMNS

PRE-WEDDING MUSIC

PROCESSIONAL MUSIC

MUSIC DURING SIGNING OF THE REGISTER

RECESSIONAL MUSIC

PHOTOGRAPHS ALLOWED

VIDEO CAMERAS

CONTACT FOR CHURCH FLOWERS

TELEPHONE

DONATION REQUIRED

NAMES OF OTHER BRIDES

OWN FLOWERS TO BE DELIVERED

TIME FOR FLOWERS TO BE DELIVERED

CHOIR ARRANGEMENTS

BELL-RINGING

SUGGESTIONS OR RECOMMENDATIONS FROM MINISTER

the minister

Civil ceremonies can take place at a register office or on approved premises. The service is shorter and simpler. It does not include any religious elements, although the couple do exchange vows.

Weddings in Register Offices

- ✧ Register offices cannot accommodate large numbers of people so generally the guests are limited to the couple's close family and friends, while a larger party can be entertained later in the day.
- ✧ The bride does not usually wear a traditional wedding dress or have special attendants.
- ✧ Not all register offices are staffed full-time. Check for details.
- ✧ Any civil ceremony must be witnessed by two people over 18 years of age.
- ✧ Make sure you fulfil the residency requirements. If you live in different districts, you must register in each district.
- ✧ You will require your birth certificates, divorce absolute certificate or former spouse's death certificate, if appropriate.
- ✧ Choose and confirm the date and time of the ceremony.
- ✧ Discuss whether you are to be married by Certificate or Certificate and Licence (see pages 164–5).
- ✧ If the bride intends to change her name on her passport, ask the registrar to sign the form PD2 which is available from post offices.

the registrar

Weddings on Approved Premises

Weddings can now also take place on other approved premises.

- ✦ The General Register Office and bridal magazines (see pages 185 and 188) will have more information on venues.
- ✦ Some ancestral homes or castles are now licensed so you can hold your wedding ceremony and reception in the house and grounds.
- ✦ Services tend to follow a similar pattern to that used in a register office and will not have a religious significance.
- ✦ Make sure you check that the service arrangements are what you want, as they may vary.
- ✦ You may be able to hold your reception on the same premises.
- ✦ Some approved premises will book the registrar for you, otherwise you will have to make the arrangements yourself.
- ✦ Expect to pay upwards of £150 for the registrar to attend in addition to the cost of the premises or at least as part of the package.

Personal Ceremonies

Some people choose to make their vows in a very personal way and arrange a unique ceremony.

- ✦ This must be in addition to a legal religious or civil ceremony.
- ✦ You can hold the ceremony anywhere, with the prior permission of the owner.
- ✦ You can include any form of words you wish or have the ceremony performed by a celebrant of your own choice.
- ✦ The best way to find out about unusual ways to celebrate your wedding is to look in the quality wedding magazines which are full of advertisements for different goods and services to add that special individual touch, such as balloon flights or firework displays.

the registrar

Civil Ceremony Details

REGISTER OFFICE OR APPROVED PREMISES:

ADDRESS

TELEPHONE

REGISTRAR:

NAME

ADDRESS

TELEPHONE

CEREMONY:

DATE

TIME

LICENCE REQUIREMENTS

LICENCE APPLIED FOR

ARRANGEMENTS FOR FLOWERS

the registrar ....

Unless your budget is infinite, invite only those people who you really want to share your wedding-day celebrations.

Preparing the Guest List

- ✧ Traditionally, the bride's mother draws up the guest list in consultation with the bride and the groom's parents.
- ✧ Decide on your total numbers before you write your list, then adjust it as necessary.
- ✧ You may want to keep a few people on the list whom you will invite if others drop out.
- ✧ You may wish to invite some guests to the whole occasion, or some to the ceremony and reception and others to an evening party.
- ✧ If you are having a register office wedding, only the wedding party will attend the ceremony.
- ✧ Decide, and make clear, whether or not you are inviting children for all or part of the day.
- ✧ Be aware of any special needs of your guests.
- ✧ Provide maps showing the ceremony and reception venues, if required.
- ✧ Make appropriate plans for guests travelling to the wedding from some distance and send out the information with the invitation. Whether or not they have somewhere to stay may influence a person's ability to attend. You may be able to offer them overnight accommodation at your own home or that of a friend, or suggest local bed-and-breakfast or hotel venues. If you intend to pay for overnight accommodation, make this clear.
- ✧ Tick off acceptances or refusals immediately they are received so that you have a clear, up-to-date record of your guests.
- ✧ Use the same list as your wedding present list.
- ✧ Always take the time to send a hand-written thank-you note to those who have been kind enough to send you a gift, however small. A printed thank-you card does not have the same effect as a personal message of appreciation.

the guests

Guest List

the guests

Name	Address & Telephone	Ceremony	Reception	Evening	Invitation sent	Accepted/Refused	Special needs	Gift received	Thank you note sent (date)	Cake sent

Name	Address & Telephone	Ceremony	Reception	Evening	Invitation sent	Accepted/Refused	Special needs	Gift received	Thank you note sent (date)	Cake sent

the guests

the guests

Name	Address & Telephone	Ceremony	Reception	Evening	Invitation sent	Accepted/Refused	Special needs	Gift received	Thank you note sent (date)	Cake sent

Name	Address & Telephone	Ceremony	Reception	Evening	Invitation sent	Accepted/Refused	Special needs	Gift received	Thank you note sent (date)	Cake sent

the guests

the guests

Name	Address & Telephone	Ceremony	Reception	Evening	Invitation sent	Accepted/Refused	Special needs	Gift received	Thank you note sent (date)	Cake sent

Name	Address & Telephone	Ceremony	Reception	Evening	Invitation sent	Accepted/Refused	Special needs	Gift received	Thank you note sent (date)	Cake sent

the guests

Wedding Gift List

Especially since many couples have already set up home, either separately or together, before they get married, most guests are happy to be guided by a gift list so that they can choose something appropriate. Allow your guests plenty of choice and personalise the list to suit your own needs. The following just gives you some ideas.

- ✧ Only send a gift list if it is requested.
- ✧ Keep one list with all the information on it to avoid duplication. Send it out with a stamped addressed envelope, if necessary, and request its return by a certain date.
- ✧ Some department stores will arrange to keep your gift list and record purchases. This is only appropriate if many of the guests are likely to buy from one store.
- ✧ Make sure there is plenty of choice on the list: a range of personal and practical items and both low-priced and more expensive gifts.
- ✧ If you are collecting a particular range of crockery or other items or have colour schemes in your home, specify these on the list. Specify details of any products where required.
- ✧ Gifts are traditionally sent to the bride's parents' home.
- ✧ Ideally, gifts are given before the wedding.
- ✧ At the reception, arrange for a small table to be placed before the receiving line so that any guest who has brought a gift on the day can leave it there until the bride and groom have a chance to open it. Make sure it is in a secure place. The best man and chief bridesmaid can take charge of the gifts and fix labels to them once they have been opened.
- ✧ Keep a note of gifts received on your guest list.
- ✧ Always remember to send a thank-you letter.

the guests

Displaying Gifts

Most people like to see the couple's wedding gif
usual to arrange a display of the gifts either
during the wedding, although this is not essenti
it is inappropriate.

- ❖ Security is important so it is best to arrange a
  display in the bride's parent's home, preferably in a
  spare room.
- ❖ Place a name card with each gift. Large items or
  gifts of money are represented by a card stating
  the nature of the gift but not disclosing amounts of
  money.
- ❖ Display the gifts attractively and separate similar
  gifts if possible.

Sample Wedding List

Depending on your circumstances, you will want to create
your own personal wedding list. The one below is just to
give you some ideas of the sort of things you might include.
Use the space to personalise the details.

For the Kitchen

- ❖ Baking tins ?
- ❖ Bread bin ✗
- ❖ Bread board ✓
- ❖ Cafetière Big
- ❖ Can-opener ✗
- ❖ Carving dish ✓
- ❖ Cheese board and knife ✓
- ❖ Chopping board ✗
- ❖ Double boiler ✗
- ❖ Egg poacher ✗
- ❖ Fondue set ✗
- ❖ Frying pans LeCreuset ✓
- ❖ Garlic press ✗
- ❖ Kitchen knives + block ✓
- ❖ Kitchen scales ?
- ❖ Kitchen tools set ✓
- ❖ Knife rack ✓
- ❖ Knife sharpener ?
- ❖ Microwave cookware ✗

Grapefruit knife

Carving fork

- ❖ Mixing bowls ✗
- ❖ Rolling pin ✗
- ❖ Salad bowl and servers ✓
- ❖ Salad spinner ✓
- ❖ Saucepans *Le creuset*
- ❖ Scissors ✓
- ❖ Spice rack ✗
- ❖ Steamer ✓
- ❖ Storage jars ✓
- ❖ Toast rack ✓
- ❖ Trays ✗
- ❖ Vacuum flask ✗
- ❖ Vegetable rack ✗
- ❖ Washing-up bowl and cleaning equipment ✗
- ❖ Wok ✗
- ❖ Wooden spoons ✗

Timer

Electrical Equipment

- ❖ Alarm clock/radio ?
- ❖ Blender ✗
- ❖ Bread maker ✗
- ❖ Coffee grinder ✓
- ❖ Coffee maker ✗
- ❖ Deep-fat fryer ✗
- ❖ Electric blanket ✗
- ❖ Electric carving knife ?
- ❖ Electric drill ✓
- ❖ Electric toothbrush ✓
- ❖ Food mixer ✗
- ❖ Food processor ✗
- ❖ Hairdryer ✗
- ❖ Hand-held vacuum cleaner ✗ *small*
- ❖ Iron and ironing board ✗
- ❖ Juicer ✗
- ❖ Kettle ✗
- ❖ Pressure cooker ✓
- ❖ Radio ✗
- ❖ Sandwich toaster ✗
- ❖ Satellite system ✗
- ❖ Slo-cooker ✓ *Big*
- ❖ Standard lamp *shade* ?
- ❖ Stereo ✗
- ❖ Table lamp ?
- ❖ Teasmade ✗

Hand whisk

the guests

- ✧ Television ✗
- ✧ Toaster ✗
- ✧ Trouser press ✗
- ✧ Video recorder ✗
- ✧ Yoghurt maker ✓

White Goods

- ✧ Cooker ✗
- ✧ Dishwasher ✗
- ✧ Freezer ✗
- ✧ Fridge ✗
- ✧ Microwave ✗
- ✧ Tumble dryer ✗
- ✧ Vacuum cleaner ✗
- ✧ Washing machine ✗

Cutlery

- ✧ Butter knives   Nice set
- ✧ Carving knife and fork
- ✧ Coffee spoons
- ✧ Fish knives and forks
- ✧ Fruit knives
- ✧ Place settings
- ✧ Salad servers
- ✧ Serving spoons
- ✧ Steak knives
- ✧ Teaspoons

Crockery   Nice set

- ✧ Butter dish
- ✧ Casserole dishes
- ✧ Coffee cups and saucers
- ✧ Coffee pot
- ✧ Cream jug
- ✧ Cruet set
- ✧ Dessert bowls
- ✧ Dessert plates
- ✧ Dinner plates
- ✧ Egg cups   4
- ✧ Flan dishes
- ✧ Milk jug
- ✧ Mugs   4
- ✧ Ramekins
- ✧ Sauce boat

- ✧ Serving dishes 2
- ✧ Side plates 6
- ✧ Soufflé dishes
- ✧ Soup bowls
- ✧ Soup tureen
- ✧ Sugar bowl
- ✧ Tea cups and saucers
- ✧ Tea pot 1

Glassware Nice

- ✧ Beer glasses
- ✧ Brandy balloons ?
- ✧ Champagne flutes
- ✧ Liqueur glasses + Everyday
- ✧ Red wine glasses 12 glasses
- ✧ Sherry glasses + jug
- ✧ Tumblers
- ✧ White wine glasses 12

Accessories for the Table

- ✧ Bottle opener ✗
- ✧ Carafe ✓
- ✧ Coasters
- ✧ Cocktail shaker ✓
- ✧ Corkscrew ✗
- ✧ Decanter ✓
- ✧ Ice bucket ✓
- ✧ Napkin rings ✓
- ✧ Table mats ?
- ✧ Water set ✗
- ✧ Wine cooler ~~bucket~~ ✓?
- ✧ Wine rack ✗ ? nice.

? w?

Linen

- ✧ Bath-mat set ✗
- ✧ Bath sheets ✓ colour?
- ✧ Bath towels
- ✧ Bedspreads ✗
- ✧ Cushions ✗
- ✧ Duvet ✗ ?
- ✧ Duvet cover ?
- ✧ Hand towels ✓
- ✧ Napkins ✓
- ✧ Pillowcases ?

- ✧ Sheets ?
- ✧ Table cloth ?
- ✧ Tea towels ✗
- ✧ Valance ✗

Furniture

- ✧ Bedroom suite ✗
- ✧ Bookcase ✗
- ✧ Cabinet ✗
- ✧ Chairs ✗
- ✧ Coffee table ✓
- ✧ Desk ✗
- ✧ Dining room suite ✓
- ✧ Lounge suite ✓
- ✧ Z-bed ✗

For the Garden

- ✧ Barbecue ✗
- ✧ Barbecue tools ✗
- ✧ Garden plants ✗
- ✧ Garden shed ✗
- ✧ Garden tools ✗
- ✧ Hedge trimmer ✗
- ✧ Hose reel ✗
- ✧ Lawn mower ✗
- ✧ Strimmer ✓
- ✧ Wheelbarrow ✗

Miscellaneous

- ✧ Answerphone ✗
- ✧ Ashtray ✗
- ✧ Bath rack ✗
- ✧ Bathroom cabinet ✗
- ✧ Bathroom scales ✓ Gordons
- ✧ Books ✗
- ✧ Burglar alarm ✗
- ✧ Camcorder ✗
- ✧ Candlesticks Table ✓
- ✧ Clocks ✓
- ✧ Compact discs ✓
- ✧ DIY tools ✗
- ✧ Fax machine ✗
- ✧ Linen basket ✗
- ✧ Luggage ✓ ?

- ✧ Magazine rack X
- ✧ Mirrors X
- ✧ Ornaments X
- ✧ Paintings X
- ✧ Picnic basket X
- ✧ Pot plants X
- ✧ Rugs X
- ✧ Shower X
- ✧ Shower curtain X
- ✧ Smoke alarm X
- ✧ Sports equipment X
- ✧ Stepladder X
- ✧ Telephone X
- ✧ Tool box X
- ✧ Towel rail ?
- ✧ Vase ✓ Glass
- ✧ Video cassettes X

Bathroom Scales

One of the early bookings you must make is the venue for the reception, be it a hotel, a local hall, a stately home, a marquee at a friend's house, or your own front room. The most popular locations will become fully booked well in advance so don't delay your decision-making.

- ✧ Choose somewhere the right size for the number of guests you intend to invite. You want your guests to be comfortable – neither too crowded nor too spread out.
- ✧ Your budget will make a big difference to the location you choose. Shop around to find the best options and compare like-for-like quotations.
- ✧ Ask for personal recommendations, look in bridal magazines or Yellow Pages under Hotels, Halls, Clubs or Marquee Hire.
- ✧ Booking early will give you more choice of venues.
- ✧ Try to select somewhere close to the venue for the ceremony.
- ✧ Make sure the facilities are appropriate for the number of guests.
- ✧ Check on car parking facilities.
- ✧ Check on cloakroom facilities.
- ✧ Do you require special facilities for elderly or disabled guests?
- ✧ Are there any restrictions on time, alcohol, smoking, dancing or entertainment?
- ✧ Make sure insurance provisions are adequate.
- ✧ Check on deposits, dates for confirmation of numbers, if appropriate, and final payment. It is unwise to settle in full beforehand in case there is any dispute over the service or facilities provided.
- ✧ Always ask for a written quotation.

the reception manager

Reception in a Hotel

Many hotels offer a wedding package which deals with all food, accommodation, drinks, cloakroom and changing facilities and services. These can save a great deal of hard work and although the overall price will be considerable, adding up the cost of all the different elements may well cost more. Ask for a list of exactly what is covered and what are the available options.

◇ Check services and prices carefully; this is not a cheap option.

◇ You need to be sure that your party will not be restricted to accommodate other guests or functions so it is best if there is a separate function room.

◇ Accommodation will be available for out-of-town guests. You could even spend your first night there. Check the prices of rooms or additional services.

◇ Make sure the hotel is large enough to cater for the numbers you require.

◇ Ask about the range of menus and prices. Find out whether there are special prices for children. Check all the things to be considered in the next chapter on The Caterer (see pages 91–5).

◇ Find out about the provision of wine for the meal and bar facilities. Will the hotel charge corkage if you bring your own wine for the meal? Check all the things to be considered in the chapter on The Bar Attendant (see pages 97–100).

◇ Make sure there are facilities for the display of presents if you require it.

◇ Find out whether the hotel can provide musicians or a disco and check the facilities for dancing.

◇ Check whether you need to provide flowers or table decorations.

◇ Ask if it costs extra to have somewhere to leave luggage and to change for going away.

... the reception manager

Reception in a Club or Pub

Usually half-way between a hotel and a hall in terms of the facilities offered, it is worth investigating local sports, social or other clubs in case they offer function facilities.

- ❖ The cost may be less than a hotel but are the facilities appropriate for your needs? Check exactly what they offer and all the facilities they have, as listed previously under Reception in a Hotel.
- ❖ You may have to organise your own catering.
- ❖ There will usually be bar facilities. Check opening times and details.
- ❖ Some pubs also have function rooms and can cater for special events, offering both food and drink in a friendly atmosphere.

Reception in a Hall

Booking a church or other hall is a relatively inexpensive option, although you then have to organise everything else separately.

- ❖ Surroundings and atmosphere vary considerably – from comfortable to chilly and badly decorated. It is important to check the cleanliness of the hall beforehand.
- ❖ You will have to decorate the hall yourself. Make sure you have access to the hall in advance if necessary so that you can arrange flowers, table decorations and so on.
- ❖ You will need to arrange outside caterers and check what preparation and serving equipment and facilities (tables, chairs, washing-up, etc.) are available.
- ❖ Arrangements for drinks will need to be made and a licence applied for if drinks are to be sold.
- ❖ Make sure there is somewhere for the bride and groom to change.
- ❖ Is there enough room for dancing?
- ❖ You will need to make your own arrangements for entertainment.
- ❖ There may not be anywhere to display presents.
- ❖ Alternative arrangements will have to be made for overnight accommodation.

Reception at Home

The most intimate option, especially for smaller groups, this does involve quite a lot of preparation work – not to mention clearing up.

- ✧ It is a friendly and informal choice with no time restrictions.
- ✧ Numbers may need to be restricted.
- ✧ Security for present-displays is not a problem.
- ✧ You will need to hire caterers or do it yourself.
- ✧ You will need to make arrangements for drinks.
- ✧ Toilet facilities may not be adequate for the number of guests.
- ✧ You may need to hire extra furniture or crockery and cutlery.
- ✧ Parking may be a problem.

Hiring a Marquee

If you have a large garden or can use a friend's garden, you may want to hire a marquee.

- ✧ Unreliable weather conditions need to be considered. Think about access through the house or moving from the house to the marquee.
- ✧ The hire company will probably provide flooring, awnings, electricity, etc. Check that everything is included in your quotation.
- ✧ Find out about heating, internal and external lighting and ventilation.
- ✧ Check whether they provide additional toilet facilities.
- ✧ Clarify the arrangements for erecting and dismantling the marquee. Make sure that the times are convenient.

Reception Information

RECEPTION LOCATION

CONTACT NAME

ADDRESS

TELEPHONE

ROOM(S) SIZE

FURNITURE

DECORATIONS

HEATING

CLOAKROOM FACILITIES

CHANGING FACILITIES

PARKING

GIFT DISPLAY AREA

DANCING/ENTERTAINMENT

LICENSING ARRANGEMENTS

INSURANCE

DEPOSIT PAID

BALANCE DUE DATE

the reception manager

There are any number of ways you can organise the catering for a wedding, from serving a finger buffet in your home to a full sit-down meal.

- ✧ The time of day you will be eating can affect the style of meal you choose.
- ✧ Think about the convenience of your guests and how long they will have to wait between meals.
- ✧ Summer and winter weddings will demand different approaches.
- ✧ Do you want a sit-down meal or a buffet?
- ✧ Don't expect children to behave well if they are hungry; they cannot. If you know they will have to wait for their meal, have some crisps, apples, biscuits or bars to keep them going.
- ✧ Colour and presentation make all the difference. I will never forget one wedding meal of chicken in gravy, boiled potatoes and cauliflower – memorable for all the wrong reasons.
- ✧ Make sure you know of any special dietary requirements among your guests.
- ✧ Personal recommendations are the best way to find out about caterers. You can also look in bridal magazines or Yellow Pages.
- ✧ Get a few comparable quotations.
- ✧ Confirm all agreements in writing, including details of deposits and final payment terms.
- ✧ It is unwise to settle in full beforehand in case there is any disagreement over the provision of services.

the caterer

Self-catering

Although caterers can be expensive, think very carefully about catering for your own wedding. It is a lot of hard work both immediately before and during the wedding and will take up time you and your mother, in particular, might prefer to spend on other things – like being with your guests and enjoying your big day.

◇ Most people who cater for their own wedding choose a buffet and this is most appropriate. You cannot really prepare and serve a sit-down meal when you are the principal guest. Look at the points below on buffets.

◇ It is usually only practical to serve cold food.

◇ Choose a menu for which you can prepare much of the food in advance and freeze it.

◇ Minimise last-minute shopping or preparation, especially on the morning of the wedding.

◇ You don't have to make everything yourself: supermarket freezer cabinets offer all sorts of special items, especially canapés and desserts.

◇ Don't forget to allow for shopping time.

◇ Get help from family and friends. Try to have someone else helping to serve the food on the wedding day itself.

◇ Plan the quantities carefully so that there is enough food for everyone.

◇ Make sure you have adequate table space and access to it for setting up.

◇ Keep safety and good food hygiene in mind during both preparation, storage and serving of the food.

◇ Find a catering hire company, if necessary, in a bridal magazine or Yellow Pages. They will be able to supply baking equipment, table linen and napkins, crockery and cutlery.

◇ Minimise the clearing up by using paper and plastic plates and cutlery. Have plenty of large sacks to collect up the rubbish. Detail some of the children to help out.

Choosing a Caterer

Professional caterers offer an incredible range of food services at a range of prices. Shop around and choose one which is appropriate to your reception and budget. Ask for references if appropriate.

- ✧ Most cater on a per-head price based on the meal or buffet selection you choose. These may be fixed menus or there may be flexibility in the choice.
- ✧ Find out whether there are special prices for children.
- ✧ Find out whether the wine is included in the package or whether there is a charge for corkage.
- ✧ Find out whether the cost includes serving staff.
- ✧ Make sure the cost includes clearing up.
- ✧ Ask for written confirmation of all the details of the booking.
- ✧ You will be required to place a booking deposit, then pay the balance and confirm final numbers at an agreed date.

Buffets

Buffets offer a more informal way to feed your guests with more flexibility on the dishes you can present. They also encourage the guests to mix.

- ✧ There is no need for too many choices of food. Remember that most people will want to try a little of everything.
- ✧ Think about the visual effects of the food so that the buffet table looks colourful and attractive.
- ✧ Divide the buffet into main dishes (sliced meats, flans, sausages, chicken drumsticks, pâtés, etc.); side dishes (rice or pasta salads, green salads); support dishes (bread or rolls, bread sticks, crackers, etc.); nibbles (cocktail sausages, dips and crudités, vol-au-vents, crisps, etc.) and desserts (fruit salad, gateaux, etc.).
- ✧ Make sure the buffet is not left uncovered or in a warm room for a long period of time.

the caterer

Sit-down Meals

A sit-down meal gives you the opportunity of offering a more formal spread.

- ✧ You can serve a hot meal if you wish.
- ✧ You do need proper table settings.
- ✧ It is essential to have staff to serve the meal.
- ✧ Guests can either be served at their table or be asked to go to a serving table to collect their meal.
- ✧ If you are serving a set menu, you must make sure you cater for any special dietary needs.

Table Arrangements

Work out how to seat your guests at the wedding reception and draw up a seating plan. Place cards are also useful.

- ✧ Even if you have a buffet, many people like to be able to sit down when they are eating, especially older guests.
- ✧ Young children should always be seated to eat a meal; trust me on this one.
- ✧ Generally speaking, the principal members of the wedding party sit at the top table and other guests at other tables.
- ✧ The traditional arrangement for the top table is: chief bridesmaid, groom's father, bride's mother, groom, bride, bride's father, groom's mother, best man.
- ✧ Whatever the arrangement, the bride's parents usually sit on either side of the bride and groom as they are the hosts.
- ✧ Start with the basic arrangement, then change it to suit you. Try to alternate man/woman and separate couples, but don't sit the best man next to the groom's mother if it is likely to cause an argument!
- ✧ If either set of parents is divorced, deal with the seating arrangements in a sensitive way appropriate to the circumstances. If parents have remarried, their new partners are usually asked to join the top table. The best arrangement for you is the one which will create the most relaxed friendly atmosphere. Don't let false protocol spoil your day.

the caterer

- ✧ Tables are often arranged branching out from the top table in a C-shape or E-shape.
- ✧ Smaller tables can be arranged café-style around the room.
- ✧ Try to alternate man/woman around the tables if possible.
- ✧ Seat together people who you think will get on well, but try to mix groups in a sensitive way so that guests can introduce themselves to other people they may not have met before.
- ✧ Never seat guests close together if you know they don't get on.
- ✧ Couples generally sit opposite rather than next to each other.

the caterer

The Caterer Information

COMPANY:

NAME

ADDRESS

TELEPHONE

NUMBER OF SERVING STAFF

PROVISION OF CROCKERY AND CUTLERY

AGREED MENU:

Self-catering Information

CHOSEN MENU:

CATERING EQUIPMENT HIRE:

NAME OF COMPANY

ADDRESS

TELEPHONE

BAKING EQUIPMENT

CROCKERY

CUTLERY

TABLE LINEN

SERVING DISHES

DATE FOR DELIVERY

DATE FOR RETURN

the caterer

The arrangements for the bar will vary tremendously depending on the style of your reception. You need to make sure that there is ample to drink, the right variety and that it is readily available when your guests require.

- ✧ Guests are often offered a sherry or glass of champagne on arrival.
- ✧ Wines or sparkling wines tend to be served with the meal, with wine and beer or spirits later in the evening. Soft drinks should be available at all times.
- ✧ Especially if the reception is carrying on all afternoon, many guests will appreciate a cup of tea or coffee mid-afternoon.
- ✧ Licensing laws are strict in the UK. Hotels or club premises will have their own licence. If all the drinks are to be dispensed free, you do not require a licence. If you intend to have a cash bar – whether your guests are paying for the drinks or you are putting an amount 'behind the bar' – then you must have an alcohol licence.
- ✧ Be sure whether you are buying drinks-only or drinks and service. The drinks may be part of a catering or hotel package. Check what you are getting for your money.
- ✧ Would there be a corkage charge if you bring your own wine to a licensed venue?
- ✧ Compare quotations and agree final details in writing.
- ✧ Does the quotation include clearing up? Is there a charge for breakages?
- ✧ Even for an informal reception, it is a good idea to have someone act as bar attendant. Try to make sure that none of your important guests is stuck behind the bar all day; ask older youngsters to help out, or organise a rota.
- ✧ Consider whether to employ someone for the occasion. Ask your local employment agency.

the bar attendant

Self-catering

Most suppliers will deal on a sale-or-return basis. Look at wholesale suppliers for lower prices.

- ✧ Order well in advance so you can make the most of possible discounts.
- ✧ Wine boxes are very convenient but not necessarily cheaper. Check both the price and the quality before you buy.
- ✧ Buy bags of ice from the off-licence; make sure you have somewhere to store them.
- ✧ Organise somewhere to store the drinks.
- ✧ Have an accessible table or bar from which to serve.
- ✧ Arrange hire of glasses at the same time; it is usually free (with a returnable deposit) if you are ordering your drinks. Make sure you have enough glasses of the appropriate types.
- ✧ You may also need water jugs, bottle-openers, corkscrews, ice buckets, carafes.

All Drinks Provided

This can be organised on a self-catering basis (see above) or by the caterers (see below).

Drinks Provided by the Caterers

Caterers will specify what they will serve and when it will be offered.

- ✧ Agree the range of drinks and make sure the quantity is sufficient.
- ✧ Make sure the drinks include water and soft drinks.

A Bar at the Reception

If there is already a bar in the hotel or reception venue, this takes away a lot of work from you.

- ◆ Make sure the bar is open when you need it and that it serves an appropriate range of drinks.
- ◆ Generally, you would provide free drinks on arrival, for the meal and for the cake-cutting and toasts.
- ◆ If you are paying for all the drinks, be aware that it is a very open-ended budget commitment.
- ◆ You may want to place a certain amount of money 'behind the bar', after which guests pay for their own drinks.

Choosing Drinks

The traditional wedding party drink is champagne.

- ◆ There are plenty of excellent sparkling wines that are perfectly acceptable alternatives to genuine champagne, which will be beyond the budget of most people. Try a bottle beforehand (perhaps for a party before the big day) so that you know you have chosen a good-quality wine. Look for Spanish cavas, which are excellent quality and much better value, or try store-label champagnes or sparkling wines.
- ◆ Many people serve red or white wine with the meal, then sparkling wine for the cake-cutting and toasts.
- ◆ Choose a wine to suit the meal, generally a dry white with poultry or fish (unless it is cooked in red wine), or a red wine with red meats or heavier meals. Ask the advice of the caterer.
- ◆ For a lunch-time meal, a lighter wine is generally a better choice.
- ◆ Always provide plenty of water with a meal.
- ◆ Always provide plenty of soft drinks for children or other guests.
- ◆ Have plenty of glasses – more than you think you need.
- ◆ If you are serving wines and sparkling wine, you will need extra glasses.

♦ Especially if you are self-catering, there is no need to provide the same range someone would expect of a professional bar. White and red wine, perhaps a beer and a few choices of soft drink is adequate.

Quantities

Allow a couple of glasses of sherry per person and at least half a bottle of wine per adult guest plus one glass of sparkling wine for the toasts.

♦ Sherry: 14 glasses per 70 cl bottle; 20 glasses per litre bottle.
♦ Wine: six glasses per 75 cl bottle; nine glasses per litre bottle.
♦ Champagne: six glasses per 75 cl bottle; 12 glasses per magnum (2 bottles); 24 glasses per jeroboam (4 bottles).
♦ Port: ten glasses per 70 cl bottle.
♦ Liqueurs: 32 bar measures per 70 cl bottle.
♦ Spirits: 32 bar measures per 70 cl bottle.

Bar Attendant Information

BAR TO BE PROVIDED BY

CHOICE OF DRINKS

WHEN DRINKS ARE TO BE SERVED

BAR STAFF

DRINKS TO BE OBTAINED FROM

ADDRESS

TELEPHONE

QUANTITIES AND DRINKS ORDERED

SALE OR RETURN

GLASSES TO BE OBTAINED FROM

DEPOSIT

TYPE

NUMBER

TYPE

NUMBER

RETURN DATE FOR GLASSES

SPIRIT MEASURES, OPTICS, ICE BUCKETS

BOTTLE-OPENERS, CORKSCREWS

WATER JUGS AND GLASSES

COFFEE AND TEA-MAKING ARRANGEMENTS

In many families, there is someone who is willing and able to make a wedding cake, and often they will also be able to ice it.

- ✧ A wedding cake is traditionally a fruit cake, although you might prefer a lighter sponge. If you choose a sponge cake, remember that a fondant icing will be better than a royal icing and that the cake will not keep.
- ✧ A fruit cake should be made well in advance and allowed to mature before icing.
- ✧ Wedding cakes are often tiered, and you will need to buy or hire columns to separate the tiers.
- ✧ A 13 cm (5 in) round fruit cake provides about 14 servings; a 13 cm (5 in) square cake provides about 28 servings. A 25 cm (10 in) round fruit cake provides about 68 servings; a similar-sized square cake provides about 90 servings. Sponge cakes provide half the number of servings.
- ✧ Allow sufficient cake for each guest to have a slice plus some more to send out to guests who were unable to attend.
- ✧ Traditionally the top tier of the cake is stored for a christening – although this tradition started in the days before family planning. Another option is to save the cake for your first anniversary.
- ✧ Cake tins can be hired from catering suppliers. You may also need to hire a cake knife or cake stand.
- ✧ Decorations for the top can be bought or hired. You can choose fresh flowers in a tiny vase, silk or artificial flowers or an appropriate decoration.
- ✧ Bakers will offer a range of cake designs at a range of prices. Choose the style you like from brochures and ask to see actual cakes, and to taste if possible.
- ✧ Confirm all the details, including delivery dates and payment arrangements in writing.

the baker

Baker Information

NAME

ADDRESS

TELEPHONE

CAKE STYLE

ICING STYLE

NUMBER OF TIERS

DECORATION

DELIVERY DATE

DELIVERY ADDRESS

the baker

You will probably want to include music in your church ceremony and as part of your party celebrations to set the atmosphere and give pleasure to yourselves and your guests. Choose music which is special to you and styles that you like, but remember that your guests may well span a wide range of ages and tastes, so a little of everything is often the order of the day. Keep the atmosphere light and celebratory.

Church Music

- ✧ Joyful music is played as the bride is about to arrive at the church.
- ✧ The music may be played by the organist or a tape provided.
- ✧ Arrival music: *Nimrod* from *Enigma Variations* (Elgar); *Coro* from *Water Music* (Handel); *Hornpipe in D* from *Water Music* (Handel); *Bridal March* (Parry); *Trumpet Tune* (Purcell); *Grand March* from *Aïda* (Verdi); *Crown Imperial* (Walton).
- ✧ Processional music is played as the bride and her father walk down the aisle.
- ✧ Processional music: *A Wedding Fanfare* (Bliss); *Trumpet Voluntary* (Boyce); *Arrival of the Queen of Sheba* (Handel); *Sonata No. 3* (first movement) (Mendelssohn); *Wedding March* from *The Marriage of Figaro* (Mozart); *Fanfare* (Purcell); *Choral Song* (Wesley).
- ✧ Music is often played during the signing of the register. Alternatively, the choir may sing a melodious song or a friend of the couple may sing or play.
- ✧ Signing of the register: *Air on the G String* (Bach); *Ave Maria* (Bach); *Jesu, Joy of Man's Desiring* (Bach); *Romanze* from *Eine Kleine Nachtmusik* (Mozart); *Benediction Nuptiale* (Saint-Saëns); *Chorale Prelude on Rhosymedre* (Vaughan-Williams).
- ✧ A celebratory tune is usually chosen for the recessional as the bride and groom lead the guests out of the church.

the musicians

✧ Recessional music: *Pomp and Circumstance March No. 4* (Elgar); *Bridal March* (Hollins); *Wedding March* from *Lohengrin* (Wagner); *Toccata* from Symphony No. 5 in F (Widor); *Wedding March* from *A Midsummer Night's Dream* (Mendelssohn).

✧ If you have particular favourite pieces of music, they obviously make excellent choices. Do check with the minister that your choice is suitable, especially if the music is secular.

Soloist or Choir

✧ While the couple are signing the register, you may like the choir to sing.

✧ If you have a friend who can sing or play, they can be asked to contribute to the ceremony.

✧ This is usually a choice of a piece of music with personal associations. Check with the minister that your choice is appropriate.

Hymns

✧ There are usually three hymns: on arrival, after the ceremony and after the blessing.

✧ An extra hymn is included if there is a communion as part of the service.

✧ Choose hymns you enjoy singing and which most of the congregation will know. Unusual hymns may be beautiful but they will not sound their best if your friends and family cannot join in.

✧ Choose joyful and celebratory hymns to suit the occasion.

✧ Hymn suggestions: 'All Things Bright and Beautiful'; 'Give Me Joy in My Heart'; 'Immortal, Invisible'; 'Lord of All Hopefulness'; 'Lord of the Dance'; 'Love Divine All Loves Excelling'; 'Morning Has Broken'; 'Now Thank We All Our God'; 'O Perfect Love'; 'One More Step Along the World I Go'; 'Praise to the Lord, the Almighty'.

Music for the Reception

- ❖ Decide whether you want live music all evening, a combination of live music and a disco, or just a disco or other recorded music.
- ❖ The larger the reception venue, the bigger the band or music system you will need.
- ❖ Think about different styles of band: orchestra, dance band, jazz or steel band, folk group, string quartet, rock group.
- ❖ Try to get personal recommendations for good local people who work in a style you enjoy. You will need to book early for the best musicians or DJs. Ask to hear a demonstration tape or see them in action.
- ❖ Check that they have good-quality equipment and will transport it to and from the venue.
- ❖ Check that the reception venue provides any equipment, electrical sockets, etc. they need.
- ❖ Talk to them about the style of music you want. Experienced musicians and DJs will be able to play a wide range of styles – whether live or on CD or cassette – and will be able to judge how their specific choices are going down with the audience.
- ❖ Choose your first piece of music to start the dancing and any special requests.
- ❖ Decide whether they are going to provide background music during the meal.
- ❖ Check whether a disco provides any special lighting effects.
- ❖ Agree start and finish times.
- ❖ Have all details confirmed in writing.
- ❖ Pay the agreed deposit and agree final payment terms. It is a good idea not to pay in full before the event in case you are dissatisfied.

the musicians

Entertainment for the Children

◇ If you have a number of children attending the wedding, it can be worth considering doing something special for them. They want to be involved in the occasion, but long conversations between family members who have not met since the last family wedding can be dreary.

◇ Some companies offer crèche services, although you must be sure that the children would be happy to be looked after by a stranger and many of them may not.

◇ If there are lots of young children, ask the musicians or DJs to include music they will especially enjoy.

◇ Separate entertainment for the children, such as a magician or a clown, can break up a long day for young ones.

◇ Try to have a separate room for their entertainment, if appropriate.

◇ If your budget runs to it, hire a bouncy castle or a ball pond.

◇ As a cheaper alternative, ask the ushers and older bridesmaids to set up some games or races to keep the little ones amused.

the musicians

Church Music Information

HYMNS
_____
_____

PRE-WEDDING MUSIC
_____

PROCESSIONAL MUSIC
_____

MUSIC FOR THE SIGNING
  OF THE REGISTER
_____
CHOIR TO SING
_____

SOLOIST
_____
SONG
_____
RECESSIONAL MUSIC
_____

ORGANIST:
_____
NAME
_____
ADDRESS
_____

TELEPHONE
_____

...the musicians...

Reception Music/Entertainment Information

DJ/MUSICIANS:

NAME

ADDRESS

TELEPHONE

DATE BOOKED

TIME TO START

TIME TO FINISH

BACKGROUND MUSIC DURING THE MEAL

RANGE OF MUSIC REQUESTED

FIRST PIECE OF MUSIC

SPECIAL REQUESTS

CHILDREN'S ENTERTAINER:

NAME

ADDRESS

TELEPHONE

CHILDREN'S EQUIPMENT HIRE:

COMPANY NAME

ADDRESS

TELEPHONE

the musicians

Every bride wants to look her best on her wedding day, and wearing a splendid bridal gown is one way to achieve that. Remember that fashion does not make a good master. Choose a dress that makes *you* look a million dollars.

- ✧ Think about the level of formality of your wedding and a style that is appropriate. Civil ceremonies, second marriages or weddings between older couples tend to be informal.
- ✧ You may be able to borrow a dress. Whether it is a family heirloom or one that has been worn quite recently, avoid being pressurised into wearing something you really do not like or that does not make you look your best.
- ✧ Ask for personal recommendations of bridal wear suppliers or dressmakers, or look for advertisements in bridal magazines or Yellow Pages. Visit local bridal or department stores and check out mail-order catalogues.
- ✧ Choose between white, cream or ivory on the basis of your colouring and what is most flattering.
- ✧ If you are wearing a coloured dress or outfit, choose the most flattering colours, not the most fashionable.
- ✧ Remember that the back view is just as important as the front.
- ✧ Bear in mind the likely temperature on the wedding day. Perhaps consider a jacket or wrap of some kind for a winter wedding.
- ✧ Make sure the dress fits well and is comfortable to wear for walking, kneeling, eating and dancing. It should still be comfortable if you gain or lose a few pounds before the wedding.
- ✧ Think about whether you prefer natural or synthetic fabrics. Check the crushability of the fabric.

the Dressmaker

Hiring a Dress

⬥ If you want something very special but have a limited budget, the best option is often to hire.

⬥ Choose your dress well in advance to get the best choice. Secure your dress with a deposit.

⬥ Obtain a written guarantee that the dress will be cleaned and ready for collection or delivery on the agreed date. Confirm all the arrangements including the final payments.

⬥ Ask whether the dress is available for a fitting with all the accessories before the wedding.

⬥ Check whether you are responsible for having the dress cleaned.

⬥ Check whether you are responsible should anything be spilled on the dress or should any damage occur.

⬥ Make sure the arrangements and timing for returning the dress are clear.

Buying a Dress

⬥ If you decide to buy, get a good idea of the range of prices you can expect to pay before you commit yourself.

⬥ Never be talked into buying a dress unless you are sure it is the right one.

⬥ Try on a range of gowns to see which styles are most flattering to your figure. Take your time, avoid peak shopping times when it may be busy, and take along someone whose opinion you trust – they should be honest but tactful.

⬥ Make sure the cost of any alterations is included in the price.

⬥ Have any delivery or fitting arrangements detailed in writing, with the deposit and payment terms for the dress.

⬥ Second-hand dresses are often advertised in local papers or at dress agencies and wedding magazines are the best source of information on second-hand designer dresses. As long as you are able to try them on and not pressured into buying, they can be an excellent and cost-effective way of buying a splendid dress at a fraction of the original price.

the Dressmaker

Making a Dress

◇ Choose a reputable dressmaker and ask to see some of their work.
◇ Make sure you have a written guarantee of the fitting dates and confirmation that the dress will be finished in good time.
◇ If you – or someone you know – is an experienced dressmaker, you may be able to make the dress yourself and make a considerable saving. Do allow plenty of time to finish well in advance and avoid last-minute hassle.

Accessories

◇ Buying the headdress and veil from the same store as the shop means that you can try them on together and make sure they complement each other well.
◇ Remember to choose an appropriate headdress for the dress. A long veil will not match a mid-calf length dress.
◇ Allow plenty of time to shop for comfortable shoes. You will be wearing them all day and will be standing or dancing for much of the time. Avoid slippery soles or very high heels which may not be comfortable or easy to walk in.
◇ Satin or fabric-covered shoes are available in bridal suppliers or dancewear shops. If you need to have them dyed, allow plenty of time.
◇ The right underwear is very important to make the dress look its best. Shop around until you find underwear that is comfortable, flattering and the right colour so that it does not show through the dress or create unsightly lines, especially if your dress is tight-fitting. Always have two or three pairs of tights just in case.
◇ Traditionally, the bride wears something old, something new, something borrowed and something blue to bring her luck.
◇ Some brides like to wear gloves or to carry a handbag rather than a bouquet.
◇ Jewellery should complement the dress and not be too overstated.

Looking Your Best

✧ You will want your hair to look wonderful and you
   need to consider how to have your hair done,
   especially if you are wearing a headdress or veil.
✧ Visit the hairdresser in advance to try out styles
   with the headdress.
✧ Remember that you will take off the headdress
   after the service but you still want to look good.
✧ Practise a natural-looking make-up which flatters
   your complexion and the style of your clothes.
✧ Resist the temptation to try new make-up. If you
   do buy something new, make sure you try it out
   before the day.
✧ Pale dresses may demand a softer-than-usual look.
✧ Wear your favourite perfume.

The Bridesmaids' Dresses

✧ The level of formality of the bridesmaids' dresses
   will be set by the bride's dress.
✧ Try to match the colouring of the bridesmaids so
   that they look their best. If you want them all to
   wear the same style and colour, choose something
   which is complementary to all of them.
✧ Try to make sure all the girls like the dresses.
✧ If they are paying for their own dresses, they
   should be allowed a wider degree of choice.

The Page Boys' Outfits

✧ Choose something which matches the general style
   of the wedding.
✧ Some people choose miniature versions of the
   outfits worn by the main wedding party.
✧ Page boys can also look cute in sailor suits, suits,
   knickerbockers or guardsmen's outfits.
✧ Do remember that they are little boys and will
   wriggle and squirm if they are not comfortable.

Bride's Dress Information

DRESSMAKER OR SUPPLIER

ADDRESS

TELEPHONE

DRESS STYLE

VEIL

HEADDRESS

SHOES

UNDERWEAR

DATES FOR FITTINGS

DATE FOR COLLECTION

SOMETHING OLD

SOMETHING NEW

SOMETHING BORROWED

SOMETHING BLUE

Bridesmaids' Dresses Information

DRESSMAKER OR SUPPLIER

ADDRESS

TELEPHONE

CHIEF BRIDESMAID:

NAME

DRESS STYLE

DRESS SIZE

HEADDRESS

SHOES STYLE

SHOE SIZE

DATES FOR FITTINGS

DATE FOR COLLECTION

OTHER BRIDESMAIDS:	1	2	3
NAME			
DRESS STYLE			
DRESS SIZE			
HEADDRESS			
SHOES STYLE			
SHOE SIZE			
DATE FOR FITTINGS			
DATE FOR COLLECTION			

Page Boys' Outfits Information

MAKER OR SUPPLIER

ADDRESS

TELEPHONE

PAGE BOY:	1	2
NAME		
SIZE		
STYLE OF OUTFIT		
HAT STYLE		
SHOES STYLE		
SHOE SIZE		
DATES FOR FITTINGS		
DATE FOR COLLECTION		

If you are having an informal wedding, the men will be most likely to wear lounge suits, whereas for a formal wedding the principal men will wear morning dress.

- ✧ Match the style of the men's attire to the formality of the bride's dress.
- ✧ If the bride has a colour scheme for the day, make sure that accessories etc. match with that scheme.
- ✧ The groom should set the tone for the rest of the men.
- ✧ Lounge suits should be comfortable and well-fitting. Allow time to have the trouser lengths adjusted if necessary.
- ✧ The principal men, if Scottish, may wear Highland dress; members of the Forces may wear their uniforms.
- ✧ Formal wear is usually hired.
- ✧ A traditional morning suit is a black or grey three-piece with a tail coat, or a black tail coat with pinstripe trousers, white collar and grey tie, silk top hat and gloves. Most brides prefer grey jackets.
- ✧ Formal accessories, such as a cummerbund and cravat, should be chosen to match the bridesmaids' dresses.
- ✧ Hats are carried by the brim in the left hand together with the gloves.
- ✧ Check the availability of hired suits, confirm fitting dates and collection dates in writing, as well as deposit and final payment arrangements.
- ✧ Confirm that the suits will be cleaned and ready for collection when required.
- ✧ Check whether you are responsible if the suits are damaged during the day.

the outfitter

Outfitter Information

NAME

ADDRESS

TELEPHONE

GROOM:

STYLE CHOSEN

ACCESSORIES

TROUSERS SIZE

JACKET SIZE

SHIRT SIZE

TOP HAT SIZE

GLOVES SIZE

DATES FOR FITTINGS

DATE FOR COLLECTION

UNDERWEAR

SHOES

BEST MAN:

STYLE CHOSEN

ACCESSORIES

TROUSERS SIZE

JACKET SIZE

SHIRT SIZE

TOP HAT SIZE

GLOVES SIZE

DATES FOR FITTINGS

DATE FOR COLLECTION

UNDERWEAR

SHOES

the outfitter

Fresh flowers are a wonderful way to decorate your wedding venues and complement your beautiful outfits. If they are chosen carefully, inexpensive displays can be just as beautiful as ones costing a vast amount more. It is very easy to spend a lot of money here, so make sure you are getting what you want.

✧ Before you start making definite plans, shop around, look at some portfolios and find one or two florists whose style, quality and prices you like.

✧ Ask for more detailed information and brochures before you make your final choice.

✧ Make sure you clearly specify your budget and what you expect it to cover. The florist may not be able to give you a final price until nearer the date when the prices of specific flowers are available.

✧ Discuss the style of bouquets and arrangements you require and any special flowers you would like included.

✧ Discuss colour-matching and provide fabric samples.

✧ Make sure you confirm dates, delivery times and arrangements, especially if the flowers are to be delivered to different locations.

✧ Find out what arrangements are made regarding the return of vases or containers.

✧ Have all details confirmed in writing, including deposits and final payment terms.

The Bouquets

✧ Match the style of your bouquet to the style of your dress. A classic, elegant gown demands a simple floral arrangement.

✧ Flowers in season will be of the best quality and value.

✧ Flowers with a particular meaning or sentimental association for you make a good choice.

✧ Think about the traditional meaning of particular flowers.

the florist

- ✧ Consider the colours of the bridesmaids' outfits and match the flowers accordingly.
- ✧ Some flowers are more long-lasting than others. Take your florist's advice on flowers that will not wilt before you get to the ceremony.
- ✧ Think about the fragrance of the flowers.
- ✧ Not all whites are the same. If you choose a white bouquet, make sure it matches your dress and it uses greenery to good effect.
- ✧ Alternatives to bouquets include a parasol, bible or prayer book, pomander or bag.
- ✧ Younger bridesmaids often carry a small basket of flowers rather than a bouquet.
- ✧ Dry or press a bloom from your bouquet for your keepsake album.
- ✧ Bouquets are delivered in good time to the bride's parents' home on the morning of the wedding.
- ✧ Buttonholes or corsages are usually delivered with the bouquets but other arrangements can be made if necessary. The best man should make sure he has them at the church in time for the arrival of the wedding party.

The Corsages and Buttonholes

- ✧ The principal men in the wedding party wear a flower buttonhole, usually a single white or red carnation.
- ✧ The bride's and groom's mothers usually each wear a corsage of a few flowers, chosen to complement the colours of their outfits.

Flowers for the Church or Register Office

- ✧ Many register offices are decorated with flowers at all times so you will not need to organise your own arrangements.
- ✧ If you do take flowers to a register office, a small arrangement is appropriate.
- ✧ For a grander church wedding, the church is decorated in an appropriate style.
- ✧ Some churches have restrictions on floral arrangements so check with the vicar.

- ✧ Main decorations are placed behind the altar, on window sills and on the pulpit.
- ✧ Pew-ends are sometimes decorated with posies.
- ✧ If you have an overall colour scheme for the dresses, continue this into the floral decorations. Provide the florist with fabric samples to match the colours.
- ✧ Some church flower groups will decorate the church for a small donation. Contact other brides getting married in the church on the same day in order to liaise on the colours and style of arrangements.

Flowers for the Reception

- ✧ Choose a style to suit the formality of the occasion. Elaborate floral arrangements on every table might suit a big occasion whereas more subtle decorations would be appropriate for a less formal affair.
- ✧ Continue the wedding colour scheme into the floral arrangements. Provide the florist with fabric samples to match blooms, ribbons, etc.
- ✧ The top table is generally decorated with flowers. Make sure this does not block the view of the guests.
- ✧ Floral decorations on other tables are a matter of choice.
- ✧ Single flower vases make stylish table decorations.
- ✧ If you use pot plants to decorate the tables, you can give them as gifts to guests as they depart, or take them home yourself.
- ✧ Some brides like to give a single flower to each female guest at the reception.

Other Flowers

- ✧ If you would like fresh flowers for the headdresses, order these at the same time to match the bouquets.
- ✧ You may like to order bouquets for the bride's and groom's mothers.
- ✧ Some brides like to have flowers to decorate the bridal car.

Flower Ideas

For Spring

Apple blossom	White/pink	Good fortune
Azalea	Assorted	Temperance
Bluebell	Blue	Constancy
Broom	Yellow/red	Humility and neatness
Camellia	White	Loveliness
	Red	Excellence
Clematis	Assorted	Mental beauty
Coreopsis	Assorted	Always cheerful
Forget-me-not	Blue	True love
Forsythia	Yellow	
Gentian	Blue	
Honeysuckle	Yellow/red	Generous and devoted affection
Jasmine	White	Amiability
	Yellow	Grace and elegance
Lilac	White/purple	First emotions of love
Lily of the valley	White	Return of happiness
Mimosa	Yellow	Secret love or friendship
Narcissus	White/yellow	Regard
Orange blossom	White	Happiness and everlasting love
Orchid	Assorted	Beauty
Spirea	White	
Tulip	Red	Declaration of love
	Yellow	Hopeless love
	Variegated	Beautiful eyes
Violet	Violet/yellow	

For Summer

Alstroemeria	Assorted	
Azalea	Assorted	Temperance
Campanula	Blue/white	Constancy
Cornflower	Blue	Delicacy
Daisy	Assorted	Innocence
Delphinium	Blue/pink/white	
Fuchsia	Red/pink	Taste
Gladiolus	Assorted	Bonds of affection
Jasmine	White	Amiability
	Yellow	Grace and elegance

the florist

Lupin	Assorted	
Orchid	Assorted	Beauty
Peony	White/pink/red	Shame
Stephanotis	White	
Stock	Assorted	Lasting beauty
Sweet pea	Assorted	Delicate pleasure

For Autumn

Alstroemeria	Assorted	
Aster	Assorted	Afterthought
Dahlia	Assorted	Pomp
Fuchsia	Red/pink	Taste
Gladiolus	Assorted	Bonds of affection
Hydrangea	Pink/blue	Boastfulness
Orchid	Assorted	Beauty

For Winter

Forsythia	Yellow	
Jasmine	Yellow	
Rhododendron	Purple/pink	Danger
Snowdrop	White	Hope
Winter jasmine	Yellow	Amiability, grace and elegance

Throughout the Year

Carnation	Red	Alas for my poor heart
	Striped	Refusal
	Yellow	Disdain
Chrysanthemum	Red	I love you
	White	Truth
Freesia	Assorted	
Gerbera	Assorted	
Gypsophila	Pink/white	
Iris	Blue	Burning love
Lily	Pink	Tolerance
	White	Purity and modesty
	Other	Majesty and purity
Pansy	Assorted	Faithfulness and modesty
Rose	Red	I love you
	White	I am worthy of you
	Other	Love, beauty and happiness

Florist Information

NAME

ADDRESS

TELEPHONE

BRIDE'S BOUQUET:

FLOWERS CHOSEN

GREENERY CHOSEN

STYLE

COST

BRIDESMAIDS' BOUQUETS:

FLOWERS CHOSEN

GREENERY CHOSEN

STYLE

NUMBER

COST

BUTTONHOLES:

STYLE

NUMBER

COST

CORSAGES:

STYLE

NUMBER

COST

TOTAL COST:

DEPOSIT

DELIVERY DATE

DELIVERY ARRANGEMENTS FOR
  BOUQUETS, BUTTONHOLES AND CORSAGES

the florist

The law does not require that a ring or rings be given in marriage, but the groom traditionally gives the bride a ring and it has more recently become customary for the bride to buy a ring for the groom.

- ✧ Always buy from a reputable jeweller or antique shop.
- ✧ You can choose from a range of rings, from a simple gold band to ornate or engraved rings.
- ✧ Remember that you will wear the rings for many years so make a careful choice.
- ✧ Platinum is the most expensive metal. Gold and white gold come in various carats: 24-carat gold is the purest but the heaviest and least durable; 22-carat gold is slightly more durable; 18-carat gold is the most popular choice as it is durable; 9-carat gold is the least expensive and most durable. Red gold is a more unusual choice, but is not as widely available.
- ✧ Most jewellers will be able to offer credit facilities; compare their rates with other alternatives.
- ✧ Shop around as prices vary considerably.
- ✧ If you buy an antique or second-hand ring, make sure you have it valued by a qualified appraiser.
- ✧ Obtain a valuation certificate for your rings and make sure they are covered by your household insurance.
- ✧ If the rings are to be engraved, check on the additional charges and that the rings will be ready in good time for the wedding.
- ✧ Ask for a detailed receipt which includes the cost, and a description including carat weight and gem description, if appropriate.
- ✧ Make sure you obtain an adequate guarantee.

the jeweller

Jeweller Information

NAME

ADDRESS

TELEPHONE

BRIDE'S ENGAGEMENT RING:

SIZE

STYLE

DATE ORDERED

DETAILS TO BE ENGRAVED

COLLECTION DATE

BRIDE'S WEDDING RING:

SIZE

STYLE

DATE ORDERED

DETAILS TO BE ENGRAVED

COLLECTION DATE

GROOM'S WEDDING RING:

SIZE

STYLE

DATE ORDERED

DETAILS TO BE ENGRAVED

COLLECTION DATE

DEPOSIT

BALANCE DUE DATE

TOTAL COST:

the jeweller

You can spend a great deal of money on personal stationery and printed mementoes for your wedding, or you can keep costs to a minimum. Make sure you know what you want before you are tempted to spend more than your budget allocation on printed napkins or other similar items. Ask yourself whether they contribute something to your enjoyment of the day before you decide to spend your money.

Don't forget that you will need sufficient postage stamps for all the invitations or letters you send out.

Decide first whether you are going to make your own invitations and stationery, use ready-printed stationery, or have the stationery printed.

- ✧ If you are preparing your own letters, shop around for attractive, quality paper. Make sure you buy enough to cover all your needs, or that you can get more if necessary. Buy matching envelopes at the same time. Allow yourself enough time to make a good job of the work and still finish on time.
- ✧ If you are buying ready-printed, you will find both the price and quality vary a great deal. The only way to find what you want is to shop around until you are happy. Make sure you buy sufficient quantities.
- ✧ If you want stationery printed to order, enquire with a few printers until you find two or three who offer a choice of the styles you like in the cost area you have allocated in your budget. If outline costs are favourable, you may only need to get a fixed quotation from one printer before you proceed.
- ✧ It looks very attractive if you adopt the same style for all the wedding stationery.
- ✧ You might like to include a suitable wedding motif such as bells, hearts or entwined initials.
- ✧ Wedding magazines have advertisements for unusual stationery by mail order, from beautiful calligraphy, Celtic or art nouveau styles to hand-painted silk or wacky designs with 'that smashing gold crinkly bit'.
- ✧ Provide a typed copy of all wording.

the printer

- ✧ Always allow time for checking proofs of any printed materials.
- ✧ Make sure everything is agreed in writing, including text, proofing arrangements, delivery dates, costs and payment arrangements.

Announcements

- ✧ You may wish to buy bridal notepaper and envelopes for personal letters

Invitations

- ✧ The style of the invitation should match the style of the wedding: a formal invitation for a formal wedding and so on.
- ✧ For a small wedding, a hand-written invitation on attractive stationery can be the best alternative.
- ✧ Printers will offer you a range of styles from highly formal and expensive thermographically printed invitations with double envelopes (one for the full address and an inner envelope simply for the guests' names) down to very simple designs.
- ✧ You may be able to choose different colours for the cards or paper.
- ✧ Formal invitations are often sent with a formal reply card and envelopes.
- ✧ Always write the names of all invited guests, including children, on the invitation so that there is no confusion as to whether children are invited.
- ✧ Make sure the wording includes: the hosts; guests to be invited; the couple; the date, place and time of ceremony; whether the invitation is to the ceremony, wedding party or an evening party; RSVP; an address for reply; dress code if appropriate.
- ✧ Send a map with the invitation if appropriate.
- ✧ When assessing quantities, allow one for each couple or family, a few extras for later invitations if you receive refusals, and one or two as keepsakes.
- ✧ For a formal wedding, anyone over the age of 18 should receive their own invitation, even if they live with their parents.
- ✧ Invitations should be sent out at least six weeks in advance. When ordering the invitations, allow at least two weeks for them to be printed.

the printer

- ✧ Wedding invitations are traditionally worded formally in the third person.
- ✧ The hosts, traditionally the bride's parents, send out the invitations and receive the replies.
- ✧ The wording you choose must be unambiguous, give all the relevant information, and suit the style of the occasion you are planning.
- ✧ The first line of any invitation should be the name of the host, so if this is the bride's divorced parents, her foster parents, godparents or step-parents, for example, then the wording of the first three lines should be changed accordingly to indicate the host or hosts and their relationship with the bride.
- ✧ The bride's surname is only normally included if it is different from that of the hosts.
- ✧ For a double wedding, the older couple are listed first.
- ✧ For second marriages, the hosts may be the bride's parents or the bride and groom and the wording should be altered accordingly.
- ✧ Strictly speaking, a formal invitation in the third person should receive a similarly formal reply. Replies should be dispatched as soon as possible so that the hosts can assess numbers.
- ✧ Some people include a reply card printed in the same style as the invitation and a stamped envelope so that the hosts bear the cost of the replies.

Invitations to the Ceremony and Reception

Mr and Mrs Ivor McBride
request the pleasure of the company of

....

at the marriage of their daughter
Joy
to Mr Guy Wright
at the Parish Church, Matcham
on Saturday 1st June 20— at 2.30 p.m.
and afterwards at the Bliss Hotel, Dunnet

RSVP
1 Downham Street
Matcham
ME7 9RN

the printer

Invitations to the Ceremony Only

Mr and Mrs Ivor McBride
request the pleasure of the company of
....

at the marriage of their daughter
Joy
to Mr Guy Wright
at the Parish Church, Matcham
on Saturday 1st June 20— at 2.30 p.m.

RSVP
1 Downham Street
Matcham
ME7 9RN

Invitations to the Reception Only

Mr and Mrs Ivor McBride
request the pleasure of the company of
....

at the reception to celebrate the marriage of their daughter
Joy
to Mr Guy Wright
at the Bliss Hotel, Dunnet
on Saturday 1st June 20— at 4.30 p.m.

RSVP
1 Downham Street
Matcham
ME7 9RN

Invitations to an Evening-only Celebration

Mr and Mrs Ivor McBride
request the pleasure of the company of
....

on the evening of the marriage of their daughter
Joy
to Mr Guy Wright
at the Bliss Hotel, Dunnet
on Saturday 1st June 20— at 8.30 p.m.

RSVP
1 Downham Street
Matcham
ME7 9RN

Invitations to a Service of Blessing

Mr and Mrs Ivor McBride
request the pleasure of the company of
....
at a service of blessing
following the marriage of their daughter
Joy
to Mr Guy Wright
at the Parish Church, Matcham
on Saturday 1st June 20— at 2.30 p.m.

RSVP
1 Downham Street
Matcham
ME7 9RN

Thank-you Letters

✦ Bridal notepaper and envelopes or thank-you cards
   may be specially printed, but many people prefer
   the more personal touch of a hand-written note.

Order of Service Sheets

These make it easier for the congregation to follow and
enjoy the service. You can have them printed or produce
them yourself by hand or on a home computer.

✦ Follow the order of the service exactly.
✦ Include the names of the bride and groom and the
   minister, the location of the wedding and the date
   and time of the ceremony.
✦ Include the title and composer of any music.
✦ Include the details of chosen readings.
✦ Print out the words of the hymns in full.
✦ Print out the words of prayers and responses in
   full if the congregation are expected to join in the
   service.
✦ Simply include 'Signing the register', 'Minister's
   address' or similar indications at relevant points in
   the service.
✦ Check the proof with the minister before printing.
✦ Fix your print run so that you have just the right
   number, allowing for the wedding party to keep
   one each as a keepsake.

the printer

Reception Stationery

Definitely for those with an extensive budget; you can have your names and the wedding date printed on almost anything at the reception. If you are having a formal sit-down meal, you may also wish to have a seating plan printed for display. Most people, however, draw up their own seating plan.

- ✧ Balloons
- ✧ Bottle labels
- ✧ Crackers
- ✧ Drink mats
- ✧ Favours boxes
- ✧ Guest book
- ✧ Match books or boxes
- ✧ Menus
- ✧ Napkin rings
- ✧ Napkins
- ✧ Paper plates
- ✧ Place cards
- ✧ Ribbons

After the Wedding

- ✧ Cake boxes
- ✧ Compliment cards for the cake boxes
- ✧ Change of address cards
- ✧ Keepsake books
- ✧ Photograph albums
- ✧ Photograph wallets
- ✧ Video cases

Printer Information

NAME

ADDRESS

TELEPHONE

INVITATIONS:

WORDING PROVIDED

STYLE

COLOUR OF CARD OR PAPER

INK COLOUR

ENVELOPES

QUANTITY REQUIRED

DATE FOR PROOFS

DATE FOR DELIVERY

DELIVERY ARRANGEMENTS

COST

DEPOSIT

ORDER OF SERVICE SHEETS:

WORDING PROVIDED

STYLE

COLOUR OF CARD OR PAPER

QUANTITY REQUIRED

DATE FOR PROOFS

DATE FOR DELIVERY

DELIVERY ARRANGEMENTS

COST

DEPOSIT

the printer

the printer ....

OTHER STATIONERY:

ITEM

WORDING

STYLE

COLOUR OF CARD OR PAPER

INK COLOUR

QUANTITY REQUIRED

DATE FOR PROOFS

DATE FOR DELIVERY

DELIVERY ARRANGEMENTS

COST

DEPOSIT

ITEM

WORDING

STYLE

COLOUR OF CARD OR PAPER

INK COLOUR

QUANTITY REQUIRED

DATE FOR PROOFS

DATE FOR DELIVERY

DELIVERY ARRANGEMENTS

COST

DEPOSIT

ITEM

WORDING

STYLE

COLOUR OF CARD OR PAPER

INK COLOUR

QUANTITY REQUIRED

DATE FOR PROOFS

DATE FOR DELIVERY

DELIVERY ARRANGEMENTS

COST

DEPOSIT

Your photographs will last for ever to remind you of your wedding day, so you want them to be special. Accepting friends' offers to take the photographs is generally not the best idea as they also want to enjoy the occasion and you cannot be sure of the results. Most guests will take their own photographs, so there will be no shortage of informal shots to add to your album.

- ✧ Ask friends for personal recommendations.
- ✧ Check the portfolios of local photographers so that you find one whose style you like.
- ✧ Ask how long they have been established and check the credentials of their photographers.
- ✧ Make sure they are members of a reputable association such as the Master Photographers' Association or the British Institute of Professional Photographers.
- ✧ Photographs should be of excellent quality, clear and sharp, and not catch people in awkward poses or include unwanted background detail.
- ✧ Many studios specialise in wedding photography.
- ✧ Find out which of the studio's photographers would be taking your photographs and ask to see a sample of their work.
- ✧ Check that there are back-up photographers and equipment in case of difficulties.
- ✧ Most photographs offer a wedding package which includes the photographer's attendance to take a specified number of photographs plus an album of about twenty photographs.
- ✧ Alternatively, there may be an attendance fee and a price per print and album.
- ✧ They may also have a package for parents' albums, and will have a standard charge for prints.
- ✧ Proofs are not usually available for the reception, but you should check when they will be available, make appropriate delivery arrangements and agree a timescale in which you will present your order.
- ✧ Find out whether there is a charge for the proofs, whether you can retain them and whether they will be overstamped.

the photographer

✧ Some photographers insist that you view the proofs at their studio. This may be inconvenient for you or for your guests.

✧ Establish who owns the copyright and negatives.

✧ Confirm dates and times in writing.

✧ Agree the fees in writing and pay the deposit in good time to secure your chosen photographer.

✧ Agree final payment arrangements.

✧ Discuss the style you want, referring to the portfolio, and any special shots you would like. If you are having the reception at home, for example, you may have a beautiful garden and want the photographs taken outside (but bear in mind that the weather may not co-operate).

✧ Many churches only allow a few photographs to be taken during the ceremony: the signing of the register and the recessional, for example. Make sure the photographer knows these restrictions.

✧ Photographers do not usually attend the reception. If you want them to attend, you must make special arrangements.

✧ Black and white photographs are more expensive than colour.

Photographs Checklist

This is a fairly comprehensive checklist of likely photographs. Personalise it to make sure you obtain the shots you particularly want, and agree your list with the photographer, otherwise he will follow his own pattern. For example, you may be horrified to think they'll want a picture of you at your dressing table! Tell them what you would prefer.

At Home

✧ Close-up of bride
✧ Full-length of bride
✧ Bride with her mother
✧ Bride with her father
✧ Bride with her mother and father
✧ Bride with her family
✧ Bride and bridesmaids
✧ Bride and page boys

- ✧ Bride and all attendants
- ✧ Bride at her dressing table
- ✧ Bride at the gift table
- ✧ Bride adjusting veil
- ✧ Bride with flowers
- ✧ Bridesmaids getting ready
- ✧ Mother and attendants leaving
- ✧ Bride leaving with father
- ✧ Bride getting into car

Before the Ceremony

- ✧ Groom
- ✧ Best man
- ✧ Ushers
- ✧ Groom with best man
- ✧ Groom with ushers
- ✧ Groom with best man and ushers
- ✧ Groom with his parents
- ✧ Bride's mother arriving
- ✧ Bridesmaids and page boys arriving
- ✧ Guests arriving
- ✧ Bride arriving with her father
- ✧ Bride
- ✧ Wedding party assembled

During the Ceremony (if allowed)

- ✧ Bride and her father walking down the aisle
- ✧ After the ceremony
- ✧ Signing the register
- ✧ The recessional

After the Ceremony

- ✧ Bride and groom at the church door
- ✧ Bride
- ✧ Bride and groom
- ✧ Bride and groom with best man and chief bridesmaid
- ✧ Bride and groom with best man and ushers
- ✧ Bride, groom and all attendants
- ✧ Bride, groom and officiant
- ✧ Bride, groom and bride's parents
- ✧ Bride, groom and groom's parents
- ✧ Bride, groom and both sets of parents
- ✧ Bride and groom with full wedding party

- ✧ Bride's family group
- ✧ Groom's family group
- ✧ Whole wedding group
- ✧ Bridesmaids and attendants
- ✧ Bride and groom getting into the car
- ✧ Guests throwing confetti
- ✧ Bride and groom in the car

At the Reception

- ✧ Bride and groom arriving
- ✧ Bride and groom receiving guests
- ✧ Bride and groom with parents
- ✧ Bride and groom with godparents
- ✧ Bride and groom with special friends
- ✧ Wedding party members during the speeches
- ✧ Bride and groom cutting the cake
- ✧ Bride and groom dancing the first dance
- ✧ Musicians or entertainers
- ✧ Bride and groom leaving for the honeymoon
- ✧ Bride throwing the bouquet
- ✧ The going-away car

Photographer Information

NAME OF COMPANY

ADDRESS

TELEPHONE

NAME OF PHOTOGRAPHER

DATES CONFIRMED

TIMES OF ATTENDANCE

PACKAGE:

NUMBER OF PHOTOGRAPHS TO BE TAKEN

NUMBER OF PRINTS ALLOWED

STYLE OF ALBUM

PROOFS INCLUDED

COST

PARENTS' ALBUMS:

NUMBER OF PRINTS ALLOWED

STYLE OF ALBUM

COST

DATE FOR PROOFS

DATE FOR PHOTOGRAPH ORDER

DATE FOR PROVISION OF PHOTOGRAPHS

TOTAL COST

DEPOSIT

the photographer

Guests' Photograph Orders

the photographer

Name	Address and Telephone	Proof No.	Qty	Cost

Name	Address and Telephone	Proof No.	Qty	Cost

the photographer

......the photographer......

Name	Address and Telephone	Proof No.	Qty	Cost

There are professional firms who specialise in filming and providing edited videos of your wedding day.

- ✦ Apply the same stringent quality rules for a photographer to a videographer. Look back at the list on pages 135–6.
- ✦ If you wish to video the ceremony itself, make sure this is acceptable to the minister or officiant.
- ✦ Visit the premises in advance to check whether additional lighting or sound equipment will be necessary.
- ✦ Check how the film will be edited and how long the final video will be.
- ✦ Clarify exactly what the video will include: arrival at the church, ceremony, outside the church, reception and so on.
- ✦ Make sure the videographer knows any special footage you would like.
- ✦ Find out whether the video will have professional titling.
- ✦ Find out whether there will be background music on the tape.
- ✦ Confirm everything in writing.

the videographer

Videographer Information

NAME
_____

ADDRESS
_____
_____

TELEPHONE
_____

DATE CONFIRMED
_____

TIMES OF ATTENDANCE
_____

VIDEO TO INCLUDE
_____

EDITING ARRANGEMENTS
_____

DATE VIDEO WILL BE COMPLETED
_____

COST
_____

DEPOSIT
_____

COST OF COPIES
_____

the videographer

Choosing a very special vehicle to take you to the church and the reception is a pure wedding luxury. If you can afford it, you can indulge yourself in a chauffeur-driven Rolls Royce, a veteran car, a stretch limousine, a pony and trap or a coach and four. But be warned – the more unusual your request, the more it will cost.

- ✧ You will need transport to the church for the bride and her father, and the bride's mother and bridesmaids.
- ✧ You will also need transport to the reception for the bride and groom, the bridesmaids and the bride's parents.
- ✧ The larger your dress, the larger the car you will need to transport you and your father without crumpling.
- ✧ The more bridesmaids you have, the larger the car, or cars, you'll need.
- ✧ Ask for personal recommendations, or follow up references, if necessary, from your chosen supplier.
- ✧ Choose a reputable firm who will supply the car you want at a good price.
- ✧ Inspect the cars inside and out.
- ✧ Find out whether the chauffeur will wear a uniform.
- ✧ Check that they have back-up cars in case of emergency.
- ✧ Find out whether they provide ribbons and flowers.
- ✧ The firm will need to know the collection point, ceremony venue, reception venue and the number of journeys each car will make.
- ✧ For most weddings, guests make their own arrangements for transport to the church and then to the reception venue, with a little help from the ushers if necessary.
- ✧ Make sure all details of venue and times are confirmed in writing, as well as the type and number of car, deposit and final payment arrangements and so on.

the chauffeur

Transport Information

CAR HIRE COMPANY

ADDRESS

TELEPHONE

CARS HIRED

CHAUFFEUR DETAILS

COLLECTION TIME

...... the chauffeur ......

There are three things which will determine what sort of honeymoon you choose: time, inclination and, of course, money! The idea of a honeymoon – the word comes from the idea of living on bread and honey for a month – is to be able to relax after all the activity of the previous few months and enjoy your time together. Even if you only have a weekend, it is worth doing a bit of planning so that you can be sure to enjoy every minute.

Time and Money

- ✧ Work out your holiday budget.
- ✧ Based on your work or other commitments, decide how long you can spend on your honeymoon and when you will go away.
- ✧ Planning the wedding away from high season will give you more choice and holidays will cost less.
- ✧ You don't need to have a two-week holiday immediately after the wedding. Spend a weekend together, then plan your annual holiday when your finances have had a chance to recover.
- ✧ You may decide to be completely different and organise stag and hen weekends before the wedding! Health farms often have special discount weekends for small groups. Some companies organise stag and hen weekends in Amsterdam and other cities, or adventure activity weekends. Look in quality wedding magazines.

Choice of Holiday

Discuss the type of holiday you would prefer and fix a style you are both happy with.

- ✧ Lazy, beach holiday.
- ✧ Sightseeing holiday.
- ✧ Camping or caravanning holiday.
- ✧ Sports or adventure holiday.
- ✧ Activity-based holiday, such as photography or painting.

the travel agent

- ✧ Walking or climbing holiday.
- ✧ How do you like to travel: car, train, plane, boat?
- ✧ What kind of weather would you like?
- ✧ Think about the location and weather you can expect.
- ✧ Decide whether you want accommodation only, bed and breakfast, half-board, full-board or all-inclusive.
- ✧ Does either of you have any special needs such as dietary requirements or a disability?

Wedding-package Holidays

From Las Vegas to Hawaii, from the Caribbean to Canada, specialist holiday companies organise the wedding and honeymoon in one, including booking venues and arranging the ceremony and the certificates.

- ✧ As well as bridal magazines, ABTA (see page 187) can provide a list of tour operators who specialise in wedding packages.
- ✧ Do make absolutely sure of exactly what is included in the package and in the costs, as the packages do vary considerably. Some, for example, expect you to organise and pay for documentation once you get there; you should be prepared for this.
- ✧ You will need to consider your wedding arrange-ments in a different light if you take this option. For example, you will probably have a much smaller guest list; if you are getting married in a beach location, a morning suit for the men and layers of white satin for the bride are probably not the best option! Forget convention and think unusual!
- ✧ Book the wedding a few days into the holiday to give you time to settle in. You may also have to meet residency requirements of up to a week before you can be married.
- ✧ Don't forget that you'll want some quality photographs to help you remember the event.
- ✧ You may want to combine this type of wedding with an informal party when you get home so that family and friends who have not been able to attend the wedding will nevertheless be able to give you their congratulations in person and join in your celebrations.

Booking the Honeymoon

Once you know what you are looking for, ask the advice of a travel agent or follow up advertisements and collect information on the options available. Go for a company which specialises in the sort of holiday you want.

- ✧ Booking early can be financially advantageous.
- ✧ Double-check that there are no hidden cost extras and have all details confirmed in writing, including deposit and final payment arrangements.
- ✧ Check on the documentation you need, especially if you are travelling abroad and will need a passport and perhaps visas.
- ✧ If the bride intends to change her name, book the honeymoon in the name that will match the passport. The form PD2 from the Post Office, signed by the minister, will be required to obtain a new passport.
- ✧ Book foreign currency, if necessary.
- ✧ Make sure you have good insurance cover.
- ✧ Have any necessary inoculations well in advance.
- ✧ Make a list of everything you want to take.
- ✧ Double-check that someone is looking after all the post-wedding arrangements, your house or flat, etc.

Final Arrangements

- ✧ Pack your cases in advance; you don't want to have to pack on the morning of your wedding.
- ✧ If you are stopping somewhere overnight, have separate overnight bags and arrange to leave them somewhere when you go off on holiday.
- ✧ Have the going-away outfits at the reception venue and make sure there is somewhere to change.
- ✧ Try to avoid having a long or rushed journey to the airport immediately after the wedding. Book into a local hotel so that you can enjoy the party and leave as late and with as short a journey as possible. Keep the location secret.
- ✧ Have all your holiday luggage at your overnight hotel, or ready to be picked up before you leave.
- ✧ Have all your holiday documentation safely stored. Often the best man looks after this.

Travel Information

TRAVEL AGENT NAME

ADDRESS

TELEPHONE

HOLIDAY DATES

BOOKING REFERENCE

DEPARTURE DATE

DEPARTURE TIME

DEPART FROM

DESTINATION

HOTEL/ACCOMMODATION ADDRESS

TELEPHONE

RETURN DATE

RETURN TIME

DEPART FROM

ARRIVAL TIME

ARRIVE AT

PASSPORT UP TO DATE

VISAS REQUIRED

INOCULATIONS REQUIRED

INSURANCE

COSTS

DEPOSIT

DATE FOR RECEIPT OF TICKETS

...the travel agent...

Most people who have to make speeches at weddings are not practised speech-makers or stand-up comedians, so there are two simple rules to a speech: keep it short and make it sincere.

- If there is no formal toastmaster or MC, the best man will take that role and call for silence.
- The bride's father gives the first speech which usually praises the bride and recalls an amusing anecdote from her past. He thanks anyone who has helped to organise the wedding and proposes the toast to the bride and groom.
- The groom thanks his father-in-law for his good wishes. He should make sure he thanks the bride's parents and his own parents and anyone else who has helped to organise the wedding. He thanks the guests for attending and for their gifts. He thanks the best man for his support and proposes a toast to the bridesmaids.
- The best man replies on behalf of the bridesmaids. He usually finds an amusing story about the groom, reads out any cards or telemessages and announces the cutting of the cake. Always vet any messages before reading them out.
- If the bride wishes, she can also say a few words of thanks.
- Look for advice on speech-making in *Mitch Murray's One-liners for Weddings* (W. Foulsham & Co. Ltd).

Preparing a Speech

- Jot down some rough ideas, then shape them into a natural progression.
- Don't make the speech too long. Be selective and include only the best.
- Never include anything risqué or anything which could possibly be offensive.
- Only include brief anecdotes if they are amusing and of interest to the audience.
- Try to avoid clichés and hackneyed phrases.

the speech-makers

- ✧ Write your speech but then refer to cue cards to guide you through rather than reading it word for word. This will give you more fluency and you will be able to react to the audience as you speak.
- ✧ Don't shuffle your notes or fidget with change in your pocket.
- ✧ Look at your audience and address them directly. Don't look down at the table.
- ✧ Avoid alcohol before you speak.
- ✧ Have a glass of water handy in case nerves make your mouth feel dry.
- ✧ Speak clearly and naturally and not too fast.
- ✧ Be sincere.

the speech-makers

This is your run-through of what will happen on the day. Don't even bother to read it if it will make you nervous! The idea is that knowing what to expect will make you feel more relaxed and enable you to enjoy the day to the full.

- ✧ You are celebrating a wonderful and memorable day in your life – enjoy it!
- ✧ Remember to take your time and absorb as much of the detail and atmosphere as you can.
- ✧ Everyone there is wishing you well and wants you to enjoy yourself.
- ✧ If there are hiccups, laugh! So the little bridesmaid dropped her flowers – who cares? You and your guests will only remember how sweet she looked when she blushed!
- ✧ Children are a delight, but they do have a low threshold of boredom, small stomachs and are likely to pick their noses. Delegate someone to have a bag of sweets, a few toys, some coloured pencils or a book to keep them going if they start to flag. Treat them right and their energy will last a lot longer than yours.

The Day Before

- ✧ Assemble cake.
- ✧ Give gifts to attendants and parents.
- ✧ Check through your schedule for the big day and make sure everything is ready.
- ✧ Lay out dress, accessories, make-up, etc.
- ✧ Ring the bridesmaids and confirm the arrival time.
- ✧ Ring the best man and check the time he is coming to pick up the buttonholes and the time he is planning to arrive at the church with the groom.
- ✧ Ring the florist to confirm delivery of the flowers.
- ✧ Ring the caterer and confirm arrangements.
- ✧ Ring the chauffeur and confirm arrangements.
- ✧ Ring the photographer and confirm arrangements.
- ✧ Have a manicure, pedicure, etc.
- ✧ Get to bed early.

on the big day

First Thing in the Morning

- ✧ Everyone should have a good breakfast and know their role for the day.
- ✧ Make sure the going-away car and outfits and honeymoon luggage are at the reception venue.
- ✧ The bride takes her time getting ready: has a shower, has her hair done, does her make-up.
- ✧ The chief bridesmaid supervises the bridesmaids and page boys and makes sure they are ready in good time.
- ✧ It is best not to put on the wedding dress until the last minute – just in case. The bride transfers her engagement ring to her right hand.
- ✧ The bride's mother receives the bouquets and flowers.
- ✧ The best man collects the buttonholes and corsages and the order of service sheets.
- ✧ The best man makes sure he has the rings, honeymoon documents, emergency taxi numbers and his speech.
- ✧ The bride's mother, bridesmaids and page boys leave for the church, either separately or in the same car.
- ✧ The bride and her father leave for the church.

At the Church

- ✧ The best man gets the groom to the church on time.
- ✧ The best man pays the ceremony fees to the minister.
- ✧ The best man hands out the buttonholes and corsages.
- ✧ The best man hands out the order of service sheets to the ushers.
- ✧ The ushers show guests to their appropriate places in the church. Single ladies should be accompanied to their seats.
- ✧ The photographer will arrive and begin to take photographs.
- ✧ The best man and groom take their places at the front of the church.

The Ceremony

- ✦ The bride's mother traditionally arranges the bride's veil before she goes into the church.
- ✦ The bride's mother is escorted to her place by the chief usher and the ushers take their seats at the back. They are the last to take their seats.
- ✦ The bride and her father and the bridesmaids and page boys assemble for photographs in the porch.
- ✦ When the processional music starts, the groom and best man stand up and take their positions.
- ✦ The bride walks to the altar on her father's right arm, followed by the chief bridesmaid, then the bridesmaids and page boys.

Places for the Processional

- ✦ The groom turns to greet the bride as she arrives at the altar.
- ✦ The bride's father leads her to the groom's left and takes a step back.
- ✦ The bride gives her bouquet and gloves to the chief bridesmaid, who lifts her veil.

Places at the Ceremony

- ✦ The wedding ceremony follows, including hymns, an address, exchanging vows and rings, and prayers.

- ✧ The minister leads the bride and groom, best man, bridesmaids and parents into the vestry or to a side table. The minister, bride, groom and two adult witnesses sign the register.
- ✧ The groom receives the marriage certificate.
- ✧ Meanwhile, the congregation may listen to the choir or a soloist, or sing a hymn.
- ✧ The bride takes back her bouquet and she and the groom lead the recessional out of the church.

Places for the Recessional

	ALTAR	
CHOIR		CHOIR

| BRIDE'S CLOSE RELATIVES BRIDE'S RELATIVES AND FRIENDS | BRIDE'S FATHER GROOM'S MOTHER GROOM'S FATHER BRIDE'S MOTHER ATTENDANTS CHIEF BRIDESMAID BEST MAN BRIDE GROOM | GROOM'S CLOSE RELATIVES GROOM'S RELATIVES AND FRIENDS |

- ✧ The guests follow the couple out of the church, give keepsakes and shower them with confetti (if allowed).
- ✧ The party assemble for the photographs.
- ✧ The chief usher should check to make sure nothing is left in the church.
- ✧ The bride and groom leave for the reception.
- ✧ The best man escorts the bride's mother and the groom's father, then the groom's mother and the bride's father to their cars to go to the reception, then escorts the bridesmaids to their cars.
- ✧ The best man then usually leaves for the reception.
- ✧ The chief usher makes sure all the guests have transport to the reception.

The Reception

- ✧ The bride's parents, as hosts, should be the first to arrive.
- ✧ The bride and groom, parents, best man and chief bridesmaid form a receiving line to welcome the guests.

- ✧ The best man takes charge of any gifts brought to the reception.
- ✧ Guests are generally offered a drink at the end of the line.
- ✧ The chief bridesmaid asks guests to sign the keepsake register.
- ✧ The chief bridesmaid and best man introduce guests to each other.
- ✧ The best man or toastmaster invites the guests to take their seats; the wedding party are seated first.
- ✧ The best man or toastmaster requests silence for the minister or bride's father to say 'Grace'.
- ✧ The toastmaster or bride's father indicates that the meal should start and the bride and groom begin their meal first.

The Speeches

- ✧ The speeches start after the meal.
- ✧ Ensure that everyone has a charged glass.
- ✧ The best man or toastmaster introduces the bride's father.
- ✧ The bride's father gives his speech and proposes a toast to the bride and groom.
- ✧ The groom gives his speech and proposes a toast to the bridesmaids.
- ✧ Sometimes the bride chooses to say a few words.
- ✧ The best man replies on behalf of the bridesmaids and gives his speech, reads any messages and announces the cake-cutting.
- ✧ The bride and groom cut the cake. The bride places her right hand on the knife, the groom places his right hand on top, then the bride places her left hand on his.
- ✧ The bride and groom may share a piece of cake while the rest is circulated to the guests.

The Dancing

- ✧ When the furniture has been cleared from the dance floor, the bride and groom's chosen music starts and the bride and groom begin the first dance.

- ✦ Half-way through, the bride's father interrupts to dance with his daughter and the groom asks the bride's mother to dance. The groom's parents and the best man and chief bridesmaid join at the end of the first dance.
- ✦ During the celebration, the bride should dance with all male members of the wedding party and family. The groom should dance with the female members.
- ✦ The best man and chief bridesmaid should circulate and dance with as many people as possible.

Leave-taking

- ✦ The best man arranges for safe decoration of the car and packs the honeymoon luggage in the car, together with a cleaning kit.
- ✦ The chief bridesmaid helps the bride to change, while the best man helps the groom to change.
- ✦ The bride and groom say their farewells and thank-yous to the guests and to their parents.
- ✦ The guests make two lines – one male and one female – towards the door with the family nearest the door. The bride and groom make their way down the line.
- ✦ The best man hands over the car keys and honeymoon documents.
- ✦ The bride throws her bouquet backwards over her shoulder to be caught by one of the female guests.
- ✦ The couple leave for their honeymoon.
- ✦ The party may continue as long as the host and hostess wish.
- ✦ At the end of the party the bride's mother looks after the cake, the wedding dress, and collects any gifts, cards and telemessages.
- ✦ The chief bridesmaid makes sure nothing is left behind by the women.
- ✦ The best man makes sure he has the groom's suit and nothing is left behind by the men.
- ✦ The bride's father settles any outstanding accounts and he and his wife are the last to leave.

There's still quite a lot to do both immediately after the party and during the following weeks. Delegate as much as you can, giving all the details of what needs to be done and when it should be done by.

Clothes

- ✧ Have your dress cleaned. The bride's mother or chief bridesmaid usually takes care of this.
- ✧ Remove the dress from the plastic bag and remove all tags, pins or tape. Leave to air thoroughly. Stuff any bouffant parts of the dress with acid-free tissue paper, cover with a washed, unbleached muslin bag and store in a clean, dry place. This is usually a job for the bride's mother.
- ✧ Pack away your headdress, veil, etc. Again, the bride's mother is usually responsible.
- ✧ Return any hired items to the supplier. The best man usually undertakes this job.

Photographs and Keepsakes

- ✧ The bride's mother usually collects or receives delivery of the photograph proofs if the couple are away on honeymoon.
- ✧ There will be a date by which print orders should be returned to the photographer.
- ✧ Arrange for the bride, bride's parents and groom's parents to select the photographs for their albums.
- ✧ Circulate the proofs to anyone else who might like to order photographs, or arrange for people to visit in order to make their choices.
- ✧ Have the video edited and copied.
- ✧ Collect copies of the invitation, order of service sheets, pressed flowers, cards and other mementoes and mount them in a keepsake book. The bride's mother collects items so that the bride can do this on her return from honeymoon.
- ✧ The bride's parents send a press report to the local paper with details of the wedding.

after the event

Gifts and Thank-yous

◇ Make sure none of the gifts is left at the reception venue. The chief bridesmaid or the best man is usually responsible for collecting all gifts during the wedding.

◇ Store the gifts safely until the couple return from honeymoon.

◇ The bride and groom should send out any outstanding thank-you letters as soon as possible after their return from honeymoon.

◇ The bride and groom should write to their parents and the rest of the wedding party to thank them for their support.

◇ It is traditional for the newly-weds to entertain both sets of parents and the bridesmaids and best man in their new home during the three months following the wedding.

The Cake

◇ If people have not been able to attend the wedding, it is customary to send them a piece of the cake so that they can share in wishing the couple happiness.

◇ Cake boxes and compliment slips will have been bought or ordered from the printer.

◇ The bride's mother usually organises this while the couple are away on honeymoon.

◇ Use the original guest list to mark the friends to whom you would like to send cake.

Suppliers and Services

◇ It would be appreciated if you sent appropriate letters of thanks to those who helped on the day, or provided excellent facilities or services.

Looking to the Future

⬦ There is no legal requirement for the bride to change her name, although it remains the most popular option. If you are changing your name or address, make sure you write to anyone who needs to know the information.

⬦ Send out personal change-of-address cards, if necessary.

⬦ You may need to change your doctor's surgery or dentist if you are moving a considerable distance.

⬦ Alter life insurance policies in each other's favour.

⬦ Make sure that house contents insurance is sufficient to cover the gifts you have received.

⬦ Make new wills; marriage automatically renders previous wills invalid.

⬦ Make arrangements for joint bank accounts, if you have decided this is what you want to do.

⬦ Plan to celebrate your first anniversary – and subsequent ones – in a special way so that you always remember your wedding day and use the anniversary to strengthen your relationship.

after the event

Change of Name/Address List

BANK

BREAKDOWN SERVICES COMPANY

BUILDING SOCIETY

CLUBS

CREDIT CARD COMPANIES

DSS

DOCTOR

DENTIST

DVLC

ELECTORAL ROLL

ELECTRICITY SUPPLIER

EMPLOYER

GAS SUPPLIER

INLAND REVENUE

INSURANCE COMPANIES

   CAR

   HOUSE BUILDINGS

   HOUSE CONTENTS

   LIFE

LOCAL AUTHORITY (COUNCIL TAX)

MAIL-ORDER CATALOGUE COMPANIES

MORTGAGE COMPANY

PASSPORT OFFICE

PENSION FUND

POST OFFICE (SAVINGS ACCOUNTS)

PREMIUM BOND OFFICE

PROFESSIONAL ASSOCIATIONS

STORE CARDS

TELEPHONE COMPANY

   MOBILE

WATER COMPANY

There are various legal formalities to consider when you are planning your wedding and they vary depending on whether you have chosen a Church of England service, a ceremony in another religion or a civil ceremony.

- ✧ Marriages must take place between 8 a.m. and 6 p.m. The only exceptions to this are Jewish and Quaker ceremonies performed under special licence or a register general's licence.
- ✧ Weddings are not generally allowed in churches on Sundays or in synagogues on the Jewish Sabbath.
- ✧ Weddings may take place on any day except Christmas Day and Good Friday.
- ✧ For a marriage to be legal, it has to be a public declaration before two adult witnesses.
- ✧ As it is a public declaration, the doors cannot be locked during the ceremony.
- ✧ One partner must have been born male and the other female.
- ✧ No person who is already married to a living spouse or is going through a divorce may marry.
- ✧ Both parties must be of sound mind and act by their own consent.
- ✧ Both parties must be over 16. If under 18, they must have the consent of their legal guardian.
- ✧ A marriage must be solemnised by an authorised person: superintendent registrars and registrars; ordained ministers of the Church of England; authorised ministers of other religions.
- ✧ The building must normally be registered for marriages.
- ✧ If marrying in a church other than the Church of England, the couple must have a licence.

the legalities

Marriages with a Superintendent Registrar's Certificate

- ✦ Both parties must have lived in their registration district for at least seven days.
- ✦ Notice of the wedding must be given to both registration districts (if they live in different districts), specifying where the marriage is to take place and giving the names, addresses and ages of the couple. A declaration must be signed that there is no legal objection to the marriage.
- ✦ After 21 days, the superintendent registrar will issue a certificate.
- ✦ The marriage can take place at any time within the next three months.

Marriages with a Superintendent Registrar's Certificate and Licence

- ✦ Both parties must live in England or Wales.
- ✦ One party must have lived for at least 15 days in the registration district in which the wedding is to take place.
- ✦ One party must give notice of the wedding to that registration district, specifying where the marriage is to take place and giving the names, addresses and ages of the couple. A declaration must be signed that there is no legal objection to the marriage.
- ✦ One clear day, apart from a Sunday, Christmas Day or Good Friday, must intervene before the superintendent registrar issues a certificate and licence.
- ✦ The marriage can then take place at any time within three months.

the legalities

Marriage with a Registrar General's Licence

- ✧ This is reserved for cases of extreme illness when it would be impossible for the marriage to take place in a registered building.
- ✧ Notice of the marriage must be given personally by one of the parties to the superintendent registrar of the district in which the marriage is to be solemnised.
- ✧ The licence can be issued immediately.
- ✧ The marriage can be solemnised in any place and at any time within three months.
- ✧ The marriage can follow a civil ceremony, or be carried out according to a denomination other than the Church of England, the Jewish or Quaker faith.

Marriages according to the Church of England

- ✧ These may be carried out after the publication of banns, the issue of a common or ecclesiastical licence, the issue of a special licence by or on behalf of the Archbishop of Canterbury, or by the issue of a superintendent registrar's certificate.
- ✧ Banns must be published by the minister of the church in which the wedding is to take place on three Sundays before the marriage can take place. If the couple live in different parishes, the banns must be read in both parishes, and a certificate of banns be given to the officiating minister. Once the banns have been published, the wedding can take place on any day in the following three months.
- ✧ A common or ecclesiastical licence may be obtained from the Faculty Office in London or from the Bishop's Register Office in any cathedral city, or from one of the Surrogates for granting licences in the diocese. One of the couple must appear in person and sign a declaration that there is no legal reason why the marriage cannot properly take place and that one or both of them have lived for at least 15 days before the

application in the parish of the church where they are to be married. The wedding can take place one clear day after the issue of the licence.

✧ A special licence is issued only under exceptional circumstances and allows the solemnisation of the marriage at any time or in any place within three months of the issue of the licence.

✧ A superintendent registrar's certificate is rarely used. Information can be obtained from the superintendent registrar if necessary.

Other Protestant Weddings

✧ Ministers of some non-conformist denominations are not authorised to register marriages and you may have to arrange for the registrar to be present at the ceremony.

Jewish Weddings

✧ The marriage can take place at any time and does not need to be in a registered building.

✧ Provided the secretary of the synagogue is licensed to keep a marriage register, the registrar is not required to attend.

Quaker Weddings

✧ The marriage can take place at any time and does not need to be performed in a registered building. You will need to obtain the appropriate form from the registering office at the Friends' meeting house where the marriage is to be performed.

✧ Present this to the superintendent registrar for the district.

Buddhist, Hindu, Muslim and Sikh Weddings

- ✧ The marriage must take place between the hours of 8 a.m. and 6 p.m. in a registered building.
- ✧ If the religious leader is not authorised to register marriages, you will need to arrange for the registrar to attend the ceremony.

Weddings in Scotland

- ✧ Obtain two marriage notice forms either in person or by post (one for the bride and one for the groom) from the register office for the district in which you intend to marry.
- ✧ Return the completed forms with your birth certificates (and divorce, annulment or death certificates if appropriate).
- ✧ One or both of you must call in person at the register office, not more than seven days before the wedding, to collect the marriage schedule.
- ✧ The marriage must be performed by a person entitled to do so under the Marriage (Scotland) Act 1977.
- ✧ Religious ceremonies may be performed in any place with the agreement of the officiant.
- ✧ Civil ceremonies must take place in a register office.

Weddings in Northern Ireland

- ✧ Church of Ireland weddings may take place after the publication of banns; by obtaining a licence from a licensing minister of the Church of Ireland; by obtaining a special licence from a bishop of the Church of Ireland; or by obtaining a registrar's certificate from the registrar's office in the district in which one or both of you have lived for the previous 15 days.
- ✧ For Roman Catholic weddings, you must apply for a licence from a licenser appointed by a bishop or apply for a registrar's certificate from the registrar's office in the district in which both of you have lived for the preceding seven days (or both districts).

- Presbyterian marriages may take place after the publication of banns only if the couple are both Presbyterian. Otherwise they must give notice of the marriage to the minister of the church in which one or both have been members for at least one month and obtain a certificate of that notice. This is given to a licensing minister appointed by the presbytery who will issue a licence after seven days.
- For Jewish and Quaker weddings, or any other ceremonies, you must apply for a registrar's certificate from the registrar's office. The marriage may take place at any time and in any place in Northern Ireland.
- Members of the Baptist, Congregationalist, Methodist and Quaker faiths may apply to the governing bodies of their respective churches for a special licence to marry at any time and at any place in Northern Ireland.

Weddings in the Republic of Ireland

- Roman Catholic or Church of Ireland weddings may be celebrated after the publication of banns, by episcopal licence, by ordinary ecclesiastical licence, or on production of a certificate from a registrar of civil marriages.
- Presbyterian weddings may take place after publication of banns or by special licence granted by the Moderator of the Presbyterian Church or by ordinary ecclesiastical licence.
- Jewish and Quaker weddings are celebrated by special licence granted by the chief rabbi or the clerk to the yearly meeting or on production of a certificate from a registrar of civil marriages.

However large your budget, it is easy to get carried away and overspend. The key question to keep in your mind is: 'How does this decision affect our enjoyment of the day?'

Always remember that this is your wedding and you should enjoy it in whatever way you wish. Don't be swayed by advertising that insists you must have all sorts of unnecessary extras – if they don't increase your enjoyment of the day, they are a waste of time and money.

This chapter will give you a few ideas if you find that you need to reduce your spending.

Miscellaneous Tips

- ✦ The prices of all goods and services vary dramatically. It does pay to shop around.
- ✦ Friends are often only too happy to offer their help if you ask. Make clear exactly what you would like them to do and whether you expect to pay them.
- ✦ Book early; the most reasonably priced venues and services are booked up a long way in advance.
- ✦ Choose a weekday wedding if your guests will still be able to attend.
- ✦ Don't spend a lot on some of the parties which other books might tell you are essential: on the engagement, after the rehearsal, etc.

The Ceremony

- ✦ Choose a register office or simple church ceremony.
- ✦ Share the church ceremony with other couples.
- ✦ Don't have a choir, soloist or bell-ringers.
- ✦ Print your own order of service sheets on your home computer.
- ✦ Time your wedding so that your honeymoon is in the off-season and therefore cheaper; or postpone the honeymoon until later.
- ✦ Choose a combined wedding/honeymoon package; the total cost could be less than an average wedding in the UK.

tips on economising

Wedding Clothes

- ✧ Borrow or buy second-hand.
- ✧ Hire, rather than buy, your dress, veil, headdress and accessories.
- ✧ Make your own dress, or ask a friend. Do make sure you have enough time and experience, though – last-minute panics are not a good idea!
- ✧ Look out for discounts if you buy your whole outfit, including accessories, from the same shop.
- ✧ Shop for your dress or shoes in the end-of-range or end-of-season sales.
- ✧ Choose a dress which you can wear again after the event, perhaps one which can be dyed.
- ✧ Contact a local design college and see if they'll take you on as a 'design project'.
- ✧ Wear loose flowers in your hair rather than a headdress.
- ✧ Make sure your going-away outfit is something that will be worn again.
- ✧ Hire men's formal wear, rather than buying.
- ✧ Choose an informal wedding so that the men wear lounge suits.

Transport and Accommodation

- ✧ Use your own car or borrow from a friend, rather than hiring.
- ✧ Choose a reception venue within walking distance of the church or register office.
- ✧ Ask a friend to drive your to your first-night destination, or hire an ordinary taxi.
- ✧ Ask friends to offer overnight hospitality to guests travelling to the wedding.

The Reception

- ✧ Limit your guest list to the family and friends who you really want to share your celebrations. Does your second cousin twice removed qualify?
- ✧ Have a small celebration at home.
- ✧ If you are marrying on approved premises, have your reception there.
- ✧ Serve a buffet instead of a sit-down meal.

- ✧ Have an intimate wedding breakfast for the immediate wedding party, then an evening party for more friends.
- ✧ Most people can't recognise a genuine champagne. Choose a good Spanish cava or a sparkling wine.
- ✧ Serve Buck's Fizz instead of champagne.
- ✧ Provide the drinks yourself and buy special offers from supermarkets or off-licences, or take a day-trip to France (but remember that some venues will charge corkage if you bring your own drinks). Buy drinks on a sale-or-return basis.
- ✧ Borrow, rather than hire, catering equipment.
- ✧ If you are absolutely sure it will not take too much of your time, do your own catering. Be very careful with this choice as you want to arrive at the day fresh and have your time with your guests.
- ✧ Bake your own cake and ice it yourself or ask a friend. Choose a sponge base instead of a rich cake (but don't try to keep it!).
- ✧ Serve the wedding cake as the dessert course.
- ✧ Play taped music rather than hiring musicians or a DJ.

Printing and Stationery

- ✧ Design and print your own stationery – invitations, place cards, menus, order of service sheets – on your home computer.
- ✧ Practise calligraphy and write your own stationery.
- ✧ Buy pre-printed, off-the-shelf stationery.
- ✧ Deliver by hand or use second-class post.
- ✧ Do you seriously want to spend money on printed napkins, matchbooks, place cards and so on?

Photography

- ✧ Ask a friend to take photographs or make a video, although don't choose someone who would rather be enjoying themselves at the party. Make sure they are happy to take on the role. Remember that results cannot always be guaranteed.
- ✧ Buy your own albums or scrapbooks and mount the photographs yourself.

Flowers

✧ Share the cost of flowers for the ceremony with other brides who are being married on the same day. Try to agree a neutral colour so they don't clash with your wedding outfits.

✧ Decorate the church yourself with flowers or potted plants, then take them home after the event.

✧ Choose flowers in season so that they are less expensive.

✧ Cut your flowers from your own garden and arrange them yourself.

✧ Arrange for the church flowers to be taken to the reception venue.

✧ Make paper flowers and decorations for the reception venue.

✧ Decorate the reception venue with balloons and streamers rather than flowers.

✧ Choose dried or silk flowers for your decorations or bouquets so that you can use them again.

✧ Carry a posy of fresh flowers or a single bloom instead of a bouquet.

The Honeymoon

✧ Choose an off-season honeymoon. (June to November in the Caribbean; June to September in the Maldives; April to July in Kenya; or winter in Europe.)

✧ Make sure you consider all the costs involved. Weigh up bed and breakfast – when you will still have considerable expense when you get there – against half-board, full-board or all-inclusive.

✧ Stay at a small hotel or guest house.

✧ Rent a holiday home and go self-catering.

✧ Book a luxury weekend rather than two weeks somewhere average.

✧ Look out for travel-agent special offers.

✧ Book a cancellation, although you'll need to be flexible about destination and you'll be busy just before the wedding, so make sure you'll have time.

✧ Travel on a weekday rather than a weekend.

Under UK law, one partner must have been born male and the other female. There are also other legal requirements relating to the relationship between the partners. The lists below give the legal terminology.

If you are in any doubt about the validity of your proposed marriage, contact the Registrar General for the area in which you live (see page 185).

The Following People May Not Marry

- ❖ Anyone whose spouse is still living and from whom there has been no divorce.
- ❖ Anyone under the age of 16.
- ❖ Anyone under the age of 18, who has not married previously, who does not have the written consent of a parent or guardian.
- ❖ Anyone who is not able to act on their own consent.
- ❖ Anyone who is not of sufficiently sound mind to understand the nature of the marriage contract.

A Man May Not Marry His:

mother; adoptive mother; former adoptive mother; daughter; adoptive daughter; former adoptive daughter; father's mother; mother's mother; son's daughter; daughter's daughter; sister; father's sister; mother's sister; brother's daughter; sister's daughter; wife's mother; wife's daughter; father's wife; son's wife; father's father's wife; mother's father's wife; wife's father's mother; wife's mother's mother; wife's son's daughter; wife's daughter's daughter; son's son's wife; daughter's son's wife.

Brother and sister include half-brother and half-sister.

A Woman May Not Marry Her:

father; adoptive father; former adoptive father; son; adoptive son; former adoptive son; father's father; mother's father; son's son; daughter's son; brother; father's brother; mother's brother; brother's son; sister's son; husband's father; husband's son; mother's husband; daughter's husband; father's mother's husband; mother's mother's husband; husband's father's father; husband's mother's father; husband's son's son; husband's daughter's son; son's daughter's husband; daughter's daughter's husband.

Brother and sister include half-brother and half-sister.

These illustrations are designed to give you just some ideas about the range of products available to you when planning your wedding. It is not an exhaustive selection – that would take a book in itself which would need to be updated on a weekly basis – but it should give you some constructive ideas which you may not have considered before.

Wedding exhibitions and the quality wedding magazines are a great source of ideas and inspiration to help you make your wedding day unique.

Clothes for the Bride

Fitted velvet bodice
with straight skirt
Buttercup Couture

Gold satin with
lace off-the-
shoulder
bodice
Ellis Bridals

Brocade
bodice with
full skirt
and train
*Buttercup
Couture*

Damask boned
bodice with silk
skirt
Buttercup Couture

Lace-topped
dress with
train
Ellis Bridals

Shoes for the wedding party *Danceland*

Bridal hats
Hatstop

Puff-sleeved dress with drop waist
Affectionately Yours

Co-ordinating dresses need not always be in the same style
Ellis Bridals

Elegance and modern styling mean that bridesmaids' dresses can be worn again
Ellis Bridals

Simple styles are often the best for tiny bridesmaids
Ellis Bridals

Light grey morning suit (left) and morning coat with grey waistcoat and striped trousers
Moss Bros

photofile

177

photofile

Black morning coat with traditional striped waistcoat and trousers (above far left); dinner suits with waistcoats (above left); lounge suit (above right); Highland outfit (above far right); white dinner jacket (below left); grey morning suit and black frock coat with striped trousers (below right)
Moss Bros

Stunning bouquet of
roses and lilies
*Lavender Green/
Keith Thompson*

Three-dimensional
preserved flower
picture
Eternally Fresh

Formal table
decoration
*Lavender Green/
Keith Thompson*

Posy-style
bouquet
Lavender Green

Three-tier cake with
contrasting
decoration
Dunn's

Tiered cake with a
cascade of roses
Dunn's

Hexagonal cake on an
attractive display stand
Dunn's

Wedgwood-style
cake
Dunn's

Traditional invitations
and stationery
Bride Print

Hand-made
invitation
Yellow Door

A WEDDING
CELEBRATION
Of
JULIE
AND CRAIG

Original and classic
designs (above left
and right)
Adrienne Kerr

Mr & Mrs Michael Read
request the pleasure of your company
at an evening reception to be held in

Putechan Lodge Hotel
on Saturday 18th July, 1998
at 8.00pm
to celebrate the marriage of their daughter

Claire Catherine Margaret Read
with
Mr Iuin Reid

RSVP
"Four Winds", Peninver, by Campbeltown, Argyll PA28 6QP

photofile

Net sweet bags
Oakdene Stationery

Fancy gift boxes
Oakdene Stationery

Bridal gifts
Oakdene Stationery

Limousine (left)
and classic
coach (below)
*Cambridge Omnibus
and Carrriage Hire*

1930s Rolls Royce
Ages Past

1965 Alvis Coupé
Ages Past

Horse and carriage
Haydn Webb Carriages

photofile

Register Offices

Registrar General for England and Wales
St Catherine's House, 10 Kingsway, London, WC2B 6JP
(0171 242 0262)
Registrar General for Guernsey
The Greffe, Royal Court House, St Peter Port, Guernsey,
GY1 2PB (01481 725 277)
General Register Office for the Irish Republic
Joyce House, 8–11 Lombard Street East, Dublin 2, Eire
(003531 6711863)
General Register Office for the Isle of Man
Finch Road, Douglas, Isle of Man (01624 675212)
Superintendent Registrar for Jersey
States' Offices, Royal Square, St Helier, Jersey, JE1 1DD
(01534 50200)
The General Register Office for Northern Ireland
Oxford House, 49–55 Chichester Street, Belfast, BT1 4HL
(01232 250000)
General Register Office for Scotland
New Register House, 3 West Register Street, Edinburgh,
EH1 3YT (01313 340380)
Registrar of the Court of Faculties (for special licences)
1 The Sanctuary, London, SW1P 3JT (0171 222 5381)

Religious Organisations

The Baptist Union
Baptist House, 129 Broadway, Didcot, Oxfordshire,
OX11 8RT
The British Humanist Association
47 Theobald's Road, London, WC1X 8SP (0171 430 0908)
The General Synod of the Church of England
Enquiry Centre, Dean's Yard, Church House,
Great Smith Street, London, SW1P 3NZ (0171 222 9011)
The Church of Ireland
Central Office, Church of Ireland House, Church Avenue,
Rathmines, Dublin 6, Eire
The Church of Scotland
Department of Communication, 121 George Street,
Edinburgh, EH2 4YN (0131 225 5722)

where to find more information...

The Congregational Union of Scotland
Church House, 340 Cathedral Street, Glasgow, G1 2BQ
(0141 332 7667)
The Jewish Marriage Council
23 Ravenshurst Avenue, London, NW4 2EE
(0181 203 6311)
The Methodist Church
Press Office, Westminster Central Hall, Storey's Gate,
Westminster, London, SW1H 9NH (0171 222 8010)
The Presbyterian Church in Ireland
Church House, Fisherwick Place, Belfast, BT1 6DW
(01232 322284)
The Religious Society of Friends (Quakers)
Friends House, 173–7 Euston Road, London, NW1 2BY
(0171 387 3601)
The Scottish Episcopal Church
21 Grosvenor Crescent, Edinburgh, EH12 5EE
(0131 225 6357)
The United Reform Church
86 Tavistock Place, London, WC1H 9RT (0171 916 2020)
or City Temple, Holborn Viaduct, London, EC1A 2DE
(0171 583 8701)

Buying Antiques

The British Antique Dealers' Association
20 Rutland Gate, London, SW7 1BD (0171 589 4128)

Useful Books to Read

The Complete Wedding Organiser and Record, Carole Chapman
0-572-02338-3
Mitch Murray's One-liners for Weddings, Mitch Murray
0-572-01896-7
Step-by-step Wedding Planner, Eve Anderson 0-572-01589-5
Your Wedding Planner, Carole Chapman 0-572-02415-0
Wedding Speeches and Toasts, Barbara Jeffrey 0-572-02410-X
Wedding Etiquette, Pat and Bill Derraugh 0-572-02409-6
Best Best Man, Jacqueline Eames 0-572-02339-1
The Best Man's Organiser, Christopher Hobson
0-572-02302-0
Save Money Buying and Selling your Home, David Orange
0-572-02337-5
Wedding Speeches, Lee Jarvis 0-572-01781-2
All these books are published by W. Foulsham & Co. Ltd

Family Planning

The British Pregnancy Advisory Service
Austy Manor, Wootton Wawen, Solihull, West Midlands,
B95 6BX (01564 793225)
The Brook Advisory Centre
153a East Street, London, SE17 2SD (0171 703 7880)
Catholic Marriage Care
Clitherow House, 1 Blythe News, Blythe Road, London,
W14 0NW (0171 371 1341)
The Family Planning Association
2–12 Pentonville Road, London, N1 9FP (0171 837 5432)
Scottish Catholic Marriage Care
196 Clyde Street, Glasgow, G1 4JY (0141 304 1239)

Housing

The Housing Corporation (for a list of housing associations)
149 Tottenham Court Road, London, W1P 0BN
(0171 393 2000)

Honeymoons

The Association of British Travel Agents Ltd (ABTA)
55–7 Newman Street, London, W1P 4AH
(0171 637 2444)

Information Services

National Wedding Information Services
National House, Freepost, 121–3 High Streeet, Epping,
CM16 4BD (Freephone 0500 009027 or 01992 576461)

Magazines

Brides and Setting Up Home
The Condé Nast Publications Ltd, Vogue House,
Hanover Square, London, W1R 0AD (0171 499 9080)
Wedding and Home
IPC Magazines Ltd, King's Reach Tower, Stamford
Street, London, SE1 9LS (0171 261 7470)
You and Your Wedding
You and Your Wedding Publications Ltd
Silver House, 31–5 Beak Street, London, WR1 3LD
(0171 437 2998)

Music

The Mechanical Copyright Protection Society
Elgar House, 41 Streatham High Road, London,
SW16 1ER (0181 769 4400)
The Musicians' Union
60–2 Clapham Road, London, SW9 0JJ (0171 582 5566)

Photography

The Association of Photographers
9–10 Domingo Street, London, EC1Y 0TA
(0171 608 1441)
The British Institute of Professional Photography
Fox Talbot House, Amwell End, Ware, Hertfordshire,
SG12 9HN (01920 464011)
The Guild of Wedding Photographers (UK)
13 Market Street, Altrincham, Cheshire, WAS14 1QS
(0161 926 9367)
The Master Photographers' Association
Hallmark House, 2 Beaumont Street, Darlington
DL1 5SZ (01325 356555)
The Royal Photographic Society
The Octagon, Milsom Street, Bath, BA1 1DN
(01225 462841)

Other Organisations

DVLC
Swansea, SA99 1BL (01792 772134)
The Passport Office
Clive House, 70 Petty France, London, SW1H 9HD
(0171 799 2290)
Premium Bonds
National Savings, Blackpool, FY3 9YP

INDEX

index

index